Sweet Dreams
of
Awakening

Sweet Dreams
of
Awakening

365 Good Night Blessings

Blessings by Amy Torres

Illustrations by Harper Wood

BALBOA.
PRESS
A DIVISION OF HAY HOUSE

Grateful acknowledgment is made to the Foundation for Inner Peace and the Foundation for A Course in Miracles.

Portions quoted from *A Course in Miracles* are from the Second and Third Edition, 1996 and 2007, respectively, published by the Foundation for Inner Peace, PO Box 598, Mill Valley, CA USA 94942.

A Course in Miracles® and ACIM® are registered service marks and trademarks of the Foundation for Inner Peace.

Cover art and interior illustrations by Harper Wood
Art Director: Amy Torres

www.amytorresacim.com

Balboa Press books may be ordered through booksellers or by contacting:

Balboa Press
A Division of Hay House
1663 Liberty Drive
Bloomington, IN 47403
www.balboapress.com
1 (877) 407-4847

Print information available on the last page.

ISBN: 978-1-5043-4274-2 (sc)
ISBN: 978-1-5043-4276-6 (hc)
ISBN: 978-1-5043-4275-9 (e)

Library of Congress Control Number: 2015916586

Balboa Press rev. date: 12/01/2015

There are no grown-ups
only God's Children
whom He Loves equally

Preface

In 2011, I started a Facebook page devoted to *A Course in Miracles*: www.facebook.com/ACIMWorkbook.

This Facebook page became an integral part of my day, a devotional practice of sorts. My efforts included posting the daily workbook lesson, reminders to practice the exercises, answering questions, offering community, and sharing inspirational music, quotations, miracle stories, and more.

Not long into its inception, I felt inspired to "tuck in" my readers before they went to sleep. This manifested in the form of a good night message.

Every night of that first year, whether I was traveling, there was a serious power outage, my home was flooded, I had a severe and mysteriously prolonged flu (all of which happened), it was of the utmost importance to me to write and post a loving good night blessing (I use the words "message," "prayer" and "blessing" interchangeably).

The response was heart-warming. Readers commented that these good night prayers soothed them after a tough day, helped them sleep, opened their hearts and minds, and inspired their souls. Having no children of my own, all my tender love poured out through these brief but potent adaptations of the central theme of every workbook lesson. *Sweet Dreams of Awakening* is a collection of these prayers. They are for you.

Each of the blessings is inspired by and derived from a lesson from the *Workbook for Students* from *A Course in Miracles* (ACIM). From the first to the 365th, the idea from the lesson of the day is distilled down to a succinct good night blessing. My role was to be a clear conduit through which they flowed with Love, Harmony and Beauty.

Sometimes, I was guided to capitalize the first letter of certain words, such as Love, Self, Truth, etc. This was to denote God qualities, to clarify when a word represented Spirit, and to acclimate the mind to its true Identity. Please enjoy what may seem like inconsistencies; I simply followed Orders and trust that He Knows best.

The benedictions prime the mind to use sleep for spiritual awakening and to accelerate the healing process every spiritual seeker undergoes. These messages also stand on their own, and can be read by anyone, whether you have heard of *A Course in Miracles* or not.

The spiritual master, Mooji, says, "The world is full of Buddhas, but they are sleeping." *Sweet Dreams of Awakening* reminds all of us sleeping Buddhas to let the Holy Spirit use ego dreams for His purpose of gently awakening us to our pure, timeless, unborn and undying, God-Self.

As ACIM Lesson 140 says:

> *The happy dreams the Holy Spirit brings*
> *are different from the dreaming of the world,*
> *where one can merely dream he is awake.*
>
> *The dreams forgiveness lets the mind perceive*
> *do not induce another form of sleep, so that*
> *the dreamer dreams another dream.*
>
> *His happy dreams are heralds of the dawn of truth*
> *upon the mind. They lead from sleep to gentle*
> *waking, so that dreams are gone. And thus*
> *they cure for all eternity.*

~Amy Torres

How to Use
Sweet Dreams of Awakening

You will receive the greatest benefits from *Sweet Dreams of Awakening* if you read the blessings with an open heart and empty mind. Be willing to be Loved by a spiritual force beyond your imagining. You will find that even though you are the reader, the blessings are being Read to you; you are awakening to your Source stirring within you.

Keep paper and pen, your tablet or smartphone, at your bedside and if inspiration strikes, don't think! Just let the words or images move spontaneously through your hand. You might enjoy using the companion journal to *Sweet Dreams of Awakening*, called *365 Miracles* (published by MindPress Media).

Also, if you are doing the ACIM Workbook, you can synchronize the blessings with the lesson of the day which you are practicing. The page numbers correspond to the workbook lesson numbers.

Either way, ACIM student or not, allow yourself to be blessed as you read – relax, breathe, and open to receiving God's Immense Love for you. Give it a try right now, using the first blessing for practice:

Good Night, Infinite Mind.

As you fall asleep this very night,
allow the possibility that you do not really know anything.
Let out a big sigh of relief as you gently realize

that nothing you see means anything.
Lay your head on God's Shoulder and
open your mind to His Infinite Knowledge.

Sweet dreams of Awakening.

Next, if you like, make the blessing yours by replacing "you" with "I" or "me" in order to "own" the Message. Read it this way:

Good Night, Infinite Mind (wow, I am Infinite Mind!).

As I fall asleep this very night,
I allow the possibility that I do not really know anything.
I let out a big sigh of relief as I gently realize
that nothing I see means anything.
I lay my head on God's Shoulder and
open my mind to His Infinite Knowledge.

Thank you for giving me sweet dreams of Awakening.

The mysterious thing about blessings, prayers, and all messages from God, is that they seem to come from outside of you, but when you truly receive them you realize the blessing lives *within* you. The moment you realize this, you also know that you *are* prayer. For prayer is simply one way of expressing your True Identity as God's Child.

"Prayer has no beginning and no end. It is a part of life. But it does change in form, and grow with learning until it reaches its formless state, and fuses into total communication with God." ~ACIM, *The Song of Prayer*

Be receptive and willing to accept the blessings *Sweet Dreams of Awakening* offers. Miracles come in countless forms and these blessings are bedtime miracles. Drink them in and discover *you are the Formless.*

Sweet dreams of Awakening

You will first dream of peace,
and then awaken to it.

~A Course in Miracles

Good Night, Infinite Mind.

As you fall asleep this very night,
allow the possibility that
you do not really know anything.

Let out a big sigh of relief
as you gently realize that
nothing you see means anything.

Lay your head on God's Shoulder and
open your mind to His Infinite Knowledge.

Sweet dreams of Awakening

Good Night, One Love.

Give all your thoughts and wishes to the One
Who knows you better than you know yourself.
You have given meaning to all you see
and that was a mistake.

Sleep receptively tonight,
opening to Correction
from the Highest Love of all.

Sweet dreams of Awakening

Good Night, Clear Mind.

Leave your day behind,
and come into this moment.
Rest your cheek on Your Father's Chest,
and rest assured He is helping you clear your mind.

Keep a perfectly open mind as you fall asleep.
Suspend all judgments and do not try to understand.
Just trust that there is a purpose beyond this world
and Your Father reminds you of it tonight.

Sweet dreams of Awakening

Good Night, Inner Beauty.

Deliver your life, good and bad, to God right now.
Place your troubles on His Doorstep,
and place yourself in His Hands.

The meaningless is outside you,
and the meaningful is within.
Let God restore true meaning to your life
by asking to be a vessel for His Purpose.

Sweet dreams of Awakening

Good Night, Peaceful Mind.

*Whatever worries you may have,
you are never upset for the reason you think.*

*There is a deeper problem that makes the world go round,
and you can be part of the solution.*

*Lay all upsets at God's Feet, and
let Him soothe your troubled mind. This very night
discover the memory of God glows brightly within you.*

Sweet dreams of Awakening

Good Night, Real Vision.

Give all your anger, sadness, fear, guilt, and loneliness
to God. Connect your mind and heart with His,
and all pain is reduced to just one belief:
that you are separate from Him.

Allow that belief to be undone as you sleep tonight.

Sweet dreams of Awakening

Good Night, Timeless Love.

This holy instant let God's Light dissolve the past,
replacing an ancient hatred with a Present Love.
Discover your true Self in His Eternal Garden.

Forget the past, forget the future,
forget the very notion of time!

Now, watch as you are gently uprooted
from all you thought you were.

Sweet dreams of Awakening

Good Night, Eternal Present.

The past is gone, and the future has not come.
But the Eternal Present beckons in Its Entirety.

Use your sleep tonight to remove all blocks to Truth.
Release the past and future, and enter wholly into
the One Timeless Thought which you really are.

Sweet dreams of Awakening

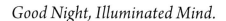

Good Night, Illuminated Mind.

Tonight, join with Spirit
and sweep the darkness away,
for understanding comes to the mind
that has been cleared of debris.

Invite the Light to dawn;
all you need do is ask
and Illumination is yours.

Sweet dreams of Awakening

9

Good Night, Full Presence.

Be willing to release every belief you hold,
and instantly you will recognize false thoughts from True.

For no matter what you think you think, or how you feel,
you have never left God's Mind and it is Here Truth abides.

Lay your head on your pillow,
and rest in God's Full Presence.
Effortlessly, all false beliefs evaporate.

Sweet dreams of Awakening

10

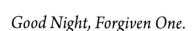

Good Night, Forgiven One.

Life without purpose is meaningless.
Forgiveness is the key to a meaningful life.

Accept God's Correction to your thinking
and peace, relaxation and freedom are yours.

Tonight, let your world be turned upside down!
You will find you are Home, where you have always been.

Sweet dreams of Awakening

Good Night, God's Word.

When you allow your thoughts to be erased,
you come to see that beneath your words
is written the Word of God.

The Word of God holds real meaning.
The Word of God is your true Identity.

Experience the Word of God tonight
and discover indescribable happiness.

Sweet dreams of Awakening

Good Night, Tranquil Mind.

Fear evaporates when we laugh at what were false beliefs.
Love heals the rift separation seems to have caused.

Stop assigning meaning to this world;
it just pits you against God.

Give up, give in, admit defeat. This is where freedom lives.
The world is meaningless until you invite
the Holy Spirit to suffuse it with God's Love.

Sweet dreams of Awakening

13

Good Night, Perfect Peace.

You are in this world, but not of it.
Salvation calls and when you listen, you are guided
in the direction of perfect safety and perfect peace.

Surrender your own private hell to God's Holy Spirit,
the memory of God within you.

God's World is Heaven, and, believe it or not,
you are at Home in Heaven right now.
So snuggle up to your Creator
and discover the peace of God tonight.

Sweet dreams of Awakening

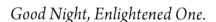

Good Night, Enlightened One.

Eyesight becomes Spiritual Vision when
you ask your Inner Teacher to lead the way.
Illumination dissolves images and illusions.

Open to Enlightenment and
allow Your Father's wise and kindly Light
to filter through and purify your mind tonight.

Sweet dreams of Awakening

Good Night, True Thought.

There is no such thing as a neutral thought.
Thoughts are either false or True.

False thoughts bring war and loathing,
uneasiness, destruction and belief in separation.
True Thought remains wholly loving and
undisturbed beneath hurtful ego fantasies.

Ease your body into bed, like a babe cozy in its cradle.
Rest in God's Heart by opening your mind to What Is True.

Sweet dreams of Awakening

Good Night, God's Vessel.

Thought is the cause of everything.
Turn your thoughts over to God and
become a vessel for His Love.

Receive and transmit
His Absolute Love, Peace and Joy.

Let His Thought pour through you tonight
*and discover you **are** His Thought!*

Sweet dreams of Awakening

17

Good Night, One Love.

What you see in others, you see in yourself.
See the Inner Light in your brothers,
and Know this Light as your Self.

Choose Love over fear, and experience
the Peace that passeth understanding.

Tonight, as you sleep, rise to Heaven, drawn
by the radiant light of Your Father's Love.

Sweet dreams of Awakening

Good Night, One Mind.

*Seeing and thinking are really the same,
and happen simultaneously.*

*Your Father's Mind is open and free,
and so is yours, for you are His Child.
He loves sharing His Thoughts with you;
nobody is left alone and separate.*

*Minds may appear to be many, but actually,
Love is extended from One Holy Mind to Itself.*

*Tonight, relax into the One Thought
and Shared Vision which you truly are.*

Sweet dreams of Awakening

19

Good Night, Vision Child.

You are learning to use spiritual vision
to distinguish between joy and sorrow,
pleasure and pain, love and fear.

Your reward is salvation, peace and happiness.
In your determination to see is Vision given you.

Accept resurrection as your birthright tonight,
and all your brothers are saved along with you.

Sweet dreams of Awakening

20

Good Night, Unified Creation.

Rest your head on your pillow
and gaze into your Father's Eyes.

Anger, hatred, fear and sadness
dissolve when exposed to Holy Light.
Let Him illuminate your mind tonight,
and so must all minds be simultaneously Lit,
for Love is Unified Creation, shared by all.

Sweet dreams of Awakening

21

Good Night, Forgiven One.

People say the best defense is an offense, yet
God Says you travel but in dreams while safe at Home.

Is it not joyous news to learn
that savage ego fantasies are not real?

Choose to recognize the eternal nature of God's Mind,
and make the happy discovery that all are forgiven.
Now you know how safe and sound you truly are!

Sweet dreams of Awakening

Good Night, Fearless One.

*This eve, allow the Holy Spirit's Vision
to turn you into a master escape artist
by practicing God's Plan for salvation.*

*Loveliness now replaces lament,
as you turn God's Key in the ego's lock
and fear dissolves in brilliant Light!*

*Oh, Fearless One, behold God's Glow
Above and Below, and know that you are That.*

Sweet dreams of Awakening

23

Good Night, Open Mind.

Lay your head on your pillow
without a care in the world.

Your Father Smiles at you as
He Strokes the hair off your forehead.
Place yourself in His Hands tonight,
and let Him clarify your best interests.

In this way, you see only the best
in your brothers and your Self.

Sweet dreams of Awakening

Good Night, Unified Mind.

Now it is time to understand your True Purpose.

As a person, you do not know what anything is for.
As God's Child, you think with His Unified Mind,
love with His Unified Heart and it is clear
that love and unity are your only purpose.

Be willing this very evening to give up
all goals you have established and trust that
when you ask Your Father to lead the way
all good things are added unto you.

Sweet dreams of Awakening

25

Good Night, Protected Child.

Stop attacking yourself in the secrecy
of your ego mind, and nestle up to Your Father.

Let Him tell you a bedtime story
of protection, safety and heavenly joy.

Let Him help you change your mind.

Sweet dreams of Awakening

Good Night, Blessed Vision.

*Child of God, you were created to create
the good, the beautiful and the holy.*

*Above all limited ego "seeing"
is the vista of True Vision which is truly blessed.*

*The physical eye is incapable of True Vision,
but ask for the Holy Spirit's blessed help, and
everything you look upon is healed and holy.*

Sweet dreams of Awakening

27

Good Night, Universal Purpose.

When you have seen one thing differently,
you will see all things differently.

God's Light will shine through
everyone and everything, everywhere.

Drop your preconceived notions. Let go of the past.
Open your mind to something beautiful, clean,
and of infinite value, full of happiness and hope.

Do this tonight and discover your Universal Purpose.

Sweet dreams of Awakening

28

Good Night, God's Visionary.

*You are beginning to look on all things
with love, appreciation and open-mindedness.*

*As you do this, you discover
that nothing is as it appears.*

*When you allow Vision to show you
what is within appearances,
holiness lights up your entire life.*

*Tonight, rest easy as you feel
the Touch of God's Loving Hand
guiding you to your Formless Source.*

Sweet dreams of Awakening

29

Good Night, One Spirit.

Real Vision is unlimited by here and there, near and far.
It does not depend upon the body's eyes at all.

God is in everything you see
because God is in your Mind.

Vision reveals we are all one big Family,
safe in the Heart of God. Join with this truth
and know your Self as One Spirit.

Sweet dreams of Awakening

Good Night, Free Spirit.

Before you fall asleep, survey your inner world.
Let good thoughts and bad thoughts surface.
View each one briefly; then let it be replaced by the next.

Once you realize you have chosen the ego as your teacher,
you are free to release victimhood in all its forms.
Choose the Holy Spirit instead and set yourself free,
for in your freedom lies the freedom of the entire world.

Sweet dreams of Awakening

Good Night, Freedom Seeker.

Your outer world and inner world are actually the same because both are in your own imagination.

Tonight, release yourself from mental bondage through your willingness to understand that you invented the world you see.

Sweet dreams of Awakening

Good Night, Heavenly One.

There is another way of looking at the world.
Look through the Holy Spirit's Vision.

When you do, everyone and everything,
everywhere, glows with Loving Light.

View the world this way tonight.

Sweet dreams of Awakening

33

Good Night, Peaceful One.

Your true inner nature is peace.
Peace is the very heart of Who You Are.
Peace of Mind is your inheritance.

Your Father kisses the top of your head
and opens your mind to this Truth,
that you may sleep peacefully in this Knowing.

Sweet dreams of Awakening

Good Night, Holy One.

Your mind is part of God's and His Loving Thought suffuses your mind with His Holiness.

Holiness is Perfect, Pure and Bright, as are You.

Simply choose to tap into your Luminous Source and surely you will shine brightly in your sleep tonight.

Sweet dreams of Awakening

35

Good Night, Enveloping Holiness.

Let God See through your eyes tonight.
It matters not that they are closed.
True seeing is holy vision and emanates
from Your Source, not your brain.

You arose from Holy Innocence and
Holy Innocence you remain. As you remember this,
you see everyone and everything as Holy as your Self.

Sweet dreams of Awakening

Good Night, Holy Light.

*Your purpose is to see the world
through your own holiness.
The Truth is, you are radiant with Loving Light.*

*All gain through your holy Vision
because It ignites the Light in everyone
and everything, everywhere.*

Thus are you and the whole world blessed together.

Sweet dreams of Awakening

Good Night, Power of God.

Your holiness is beyond space, time,
distance and limits of any kind.

You are holy because you are as God created you:
Infinite, Innocent, Pure, Unified, Loving, and Joyous.

Your holiness heals and releases the world.
Align with the Power of God within you tonight!

Sweet dreams of Awakening

38

Good Night, Holy Savior.

Your holiness is the answer
to every question that was ever asked,
is being asked now, or will be asked in the future.

Your holiness shines away separation,
darkness, guilt, and fear.
Your holiness is the salvation of the world,
and therefore your own, for a savior must be saved.

Simply ask for salvation this very night
and discover Heaven is your Home.

Sweet dreams of Awakening

39

Good Night, Son of God.

You are blessed as a Son of God,
so you are happy, peaceful, loving and content.

You are blessed as a Daughter of God,
so you are calm, quiet, assured and confident.

Lay your head on Your Father's Shoulder,
Child of God, and accept all His blessings.

Sweet dreams of Awakening

40

Good Night, God's Child.

God is within your reach,
because there is no distance
between you and Your Father.

As you fall asleep tonight,
sink down and inward and
discover your Constant Companion,
for God goes with you wherever you go.

Sweet dreams of Awakening

41

Good Night, Gifted One.

God is your strength. Vision is His gift to you.

This gift is always available, but you must be receptive.
As you fall asleep tonight, repeat to yourself,
"God is my strength. Vision is His gift."

Let related thoughts arise in your mind.
You may be astonished at how rewarding they are!

Sweet dreams of Awakening

Good Night, God-Mind.

God is your Source.
His realm of Knowledge is His Loving Heart.
His Holy Spirit lives within you and can restore
*His Vision to your awareness, **if you ask.***

Request that the Holy Spirit purify your mind tonight,
that you may truly see with Him Who is your Source.

Sweet dreams of Awakening

43

Good Night, Shining Light.

Leave behind everything you now believe,
and enter into the truth of God's Light.

The ego objects, but pay it no mind
for there is nothing to fear. Permit your mind
to take its natural course; just let go and follow.

God is the Light in which you See.
Relax and be enveloped by the Shining Light.

Sweet dreams of Awakening

Good Night, Holy Mind.

*Tonight, we aim high in order to remember
we are already at Home in the Mind of God.*

*God is the Mind with which we think.
God is the Heart with which we Love.
Your mind is joined with the Mind of God.*

*Be confident you are Holy and say,
"Thank You and Amen!"*

Sweet dreams of Awakening

45

Good Night, Forgiven One.

God is the Love in which you forgive and are forgiven.
*There is only One Son, **You**, and it is time to stop attacking.*

Forgiveness undoes what fear has produced and
all that is left is Freedom! Uncover your Harmonious Self
*and realize tonight that all is forgiven for You **are** Love.*

Sweet dreams of Awakening

46

Good Night, Love Power.

Confidence lies in trusting God and not yourself.

Tonight, slip past all your concerns and weaknesses
by reaching deep down into your mind
where there is a place of real safety and perfect peace.

Here, nothing is impossible.
Here, the strength of God abides.
His Strength is yours, if you choose It.

Sweet dreams of Awakening

Good Night, Fearless One.

Trusting in your own strength will never ease your fears.
But leaning on God will surely relieve your heart
of every terror that ever gripped it.

His Gentle Inner Strength is your Fearless Inner Peace.
Be willing to accept that there is nothing to fear
and watch fiction turn to Fact this very instant.

Sweet dreams of Awakening

Good Night, Still Self.

Have faith that the part of your mind in which Truth abides
is in constant communication with God,
whether you are aware of it or not.

Just rest your head on your pillow and hear God's Voice
call to you Lovingly. Sink deeply into the Stillness
and Silence where Peace reigns forever.
Listen to Your Father.

Sweet dreams of Awakening

49

Good Night, God's Love.

Tonight, allow God's Peace to flow over you
like a blanket of protection and surety.

Rest in your Father's Arms,
cozy in the Kingdom of Heaven,
knowing God transports you beyond every sorrow.
For you are sustained by the Love of God,
eternal, changeless and forever unfailing.

Sweet dreams of Awakening

Good Night, God's Creation.

*Place your weary head in Your Father's Hands
in full certainty that He will make sense
of this crazy, misbegotten world for you.*

*Let Him give your life meaning. Just ask,
"Father, can you please give my life purpose?"
and He will Answer. Receive His Reply tonight.*

Sweet dreams of Awakening

Good Night, Timeless One.

Reality brings Perfect Peace.

*As you allow forgiveness
to release the past and heal your mind,
you bless everyone and everyone blesses you.*

Elect to forgive and remember You are Timeless.

Sweet dreams of Awakening

52

Good Night, Beneficent Light.

You have hidden Your Identity behind clouds of madness.
Withdraw your belief in meaningless illusions and
discover you are within God's Beneficent Light.

Tonight, walk through this seemingly blinding fog
into the Golden Presence on the other side and
encounter your Self: radiant, glowing, alive and well!

Sweet dreams of Awakening

53

Good Night, Real Thought.

Behold the proof that what has been done through you has enabled Love to replace fear, laughter to replace tears, and abundance to replace loss.

Tonight, abandon illusions and look upon the real world, a place-less space of Love, Harmony and Beauty.

How can it be otherwise?
For your will and the Will of your Father are One.

Sweet dreams of Awakening

54

Good Night, Loving Thought.

*Open your mind to the world's real purpose
by withdrawing the one you have given it, and
learn the truth about who you are and what you see.*

*Forgiveness allows Love to return to your awareness.
The world you think you live in is nothing
compared to your Heavenly Abode.
Come Home tonight.*

Sweet dreams of Awakening

Good Night, Pure Truth.

Your Father has kept your inheritance safe for you.

It is there to be claimed whenever you choose.
Perfect security, complete fulfillment,
sweet charity and limitless love are yours.

To remember where you put them,
open your mind as you close your eyes.

Sweet dreams of Awakening

Good Night, Peaceful One.

As you realize you are not a victim of the world you see, your self-imposed chains drop away, and what seemed like prison is transformed by God's Light and Love.

Now, the world you look upon takes on the Light of forgiveness, and shines forgiveness back at you.

Tonight, accept the Peace that abides in your holy heart.

Sweet dreams of Awakening

57

Good Night, Blessed One.

Your holiness is unlimited in its power to heal,
because it is unlimited in its power to save.

What is there to be saved from except illusions?
And what are all illusions except false ideas?

Accept your Infinite Innocence
for yourself and all your brothers.
Accept Your Father's boundless support,
impeccable guidance and countless blessings for All.

Sweet dreams of Awakening

58

Good Night, Christ Mind.

God glows within you and shines His strength through you.
His Light is your Source; His Mind is your Knowledge;
His Heart beats in tune with yours.

God goes with you wherever you go,
whether you know He is with you or not.
Trust in this and welcome the happy world
His Vision shows you.

Sweet dreams of Awakening

Good Night, Love's Child.

As you forgive, you remember your Source
and the strength of Love stirs within you.
The world looks safe when seen through forgiving eyes;
forgiveness is the reflection of God's Love on earth.

Let your thoughts and your actions
be guided by Your Father. As you walk steadily
towards Truth, you will find there is nothing to fear,
for you are sustained by the Love of God.

Sweet dreams of Awakening

60

Good Night, True Light.

You are the Light of the world.
True humility requires that you accept this.

It takes humility, not arrogance,
to assume your rightful place
in God's Plan for salvation.

Glow with your natural resplendence
and discover your Inner Light tonight.

Sweet dreams of Awakening

Good Night, Happy Love.

When you are willing to accept forgiveness
as your function, your presence sparkles,
for you are the Light of the world.

Forgiveness returns the sweet and loving Truth
about your Self to your awareness.
Forgiveness is freedom from all pain and suffering, and
reveals that at your Source you are light-hearted and happy.

Light up your mind as darkness falls by saying,
"I would forgive that I may be happy."

Sweet dreams of Awakening

62

Good Night, Holy Light.

*Holy are you who have the power
to bring peace to every mind!*

*Blessed are you who come to recognize
the means for letting this be done through you.*

*Forgiveness is the means, salvation its end.
Your brothers look to you for redemption.*

*Ask Your Father to save you from yourself,
that salvation may be yours to give and receive.*

Sweet dreams of Awakening

Good Night, Savior of the World.

Your function is to forgive your brother
and, in so doing, forgive yourself.
This is salvation.

The forgiven are lit from within and
cannot help but emanate the Light which
expresses your true nature: Inner Happiness.

Forgiveness is undoing and undoing gives happiness.
You need not understand; just be willing to embrace,
"Let me forgive and be happy."

Sweet dreams of Awakening

Good Night, Clean Slate.

The full acceptance of salvation as your only function offers you escape from all your perceived difficulties.

Salvation places the key to the Door of Peace, which you have closed upon yourself, in your own hands.

It gives you the Answer to all the searching you have done since time began.

Tonight, let your mind be a clean slate on which your true function is written for you.

Sweet dreams of Awakening

Good Night, Happy Truth.

Tonight, let yourself know that happiness,
and nothing else, is your true state of Mind.

If you listen to the ego, this will seem impossible
but rely on the Holy Spirit and the truth is inarguable.

God gives you only happiness.
This is the function he has given you.
Therefore, your function and your happiness
are One, because Your Father has given you both!

Sweet dreams of Awakening

66

Good Night, Love's Creation.

Love created you like Itself:
You are the light of the world.
You are your brother's savior.
You are part of God's definition of Himself.

Holiness created you holy.
Kindness created you kind.
Perfection created you perfect.

Tonight, sink beneath distracting ego thoughts
and arrive in the blazing light of Love
in which you see yourself as Love created you.

Sweet dreams of Awakening

Good Night, Harmless Self.

As you go to bed tonight,
be completely at peace
with everyone and everything;
safe in a world that loves you,
and that you love in return.

Your Father's protection envelops you.
Know, in this holy instant,
that nothing can harm you because
when you let all your grievances go,
you discover you are blessedly safe.

Sweet dreams of Awakening

Good Night, Brilliant Light.

Be willing to see past the veil of darkness
that obscures your Luminous Self.

Release your grievances and
reveal the brilliant Light that lives within you.

Ancient tears of sorrow become light-hearted tears of Joy
when you invite God Himself to raise you up from darkness.

Sweet dreams of Awakening

69

Good Night, Loving Savior.

When you accept God's Love, you spread God's Love.
The Love you see in your brothers is the Love you are.

Salvation comes from you because
you can never completely obscure the Fact
that the impossible never occurred.

Beyond all distorted ego fantasies is the simple Truth:
you want to be healed and happy.

Take hold of Jesus' hand,
and let Him guide you through the clouds
into the Light beyond.

Sweet dreams of Awakening

70

Good Night, Devoted Child.

Only God's plan for salvation will lead to release and joy.
Do not listen when the ego claims otherwise.

Put Your Father in charge and do what He says.

Tonight, before you fall asleep, ask with sincerity,
"What would You have me do?
Where would You have me go?
What would You have me say, and to whom?"

Sweet dreams of Awakening

71

Good Night, Ethereal One.

To be without a body is to be in your natural state.
The Light of Truth is in us, where It was placed by God.

Grievances are based on form.
Tonight, recognize you are the Formless Light of Truth.
Ask, "What is salvation, Father?
I do not know. Tell me, that I may understand."

Then close your eyes and wait in quiet for His Answer.

Sweet dreams of Awakening

72

Good Night, Effulgent One.

Be willing to look upon the Light in you
and you are saved. Salvation is for you.

The ego stands powerless when you admit your Will is free!
Then it is seen that nothing can prevail
against the effulgent light of Love.

Say, with gentle firmness and quiet certainty,
"Let me behold the light that reflects God's Will and mine."
Now it becomes clear that you are united with your Self.

Sweet dreams of Awakening

Good Night, Willing One.

God's Will is the only Will.
When you recognize this,
you have recognized that your will is His.

Peace replaces the strange idea
that you are separate from God,
torn by conflicts and grievances.

Close your eyes, let Him clear your mind,
and sink into a deep sense of joy and peace
as you accept what Your Father Wills for you.

Sweet dreams of Awakening

Good Night, Love Light.

Tonight, we celebrate the happy ending
to your long dream of disaster. The Light has come,
for you have been willing to forgive the world.

Love has washed your mind clean, and
Heaven's Reflection shines away the ego's dark eyesight.

Rejoice in the power of forgiveness
to heal your sight completely.
Thank God, the Light has come!

Sweet dreams of Awakening

Good Night, God's Channel.

Tonight, dismiss all foolish ego beliefs and
hold your mind in silent readiness to hear the Voice
of Truth speak to you: "There are no laws but God's."

Open as channel to Spirit, and Joy is endlessly increased.
Listen attentively as you close your eyes,
and understand that you are Free,
for there are no laws but God's.

Sweet dreams of Awakening

Good Night, Miracle Worker.

As your eyelids grow heavy,
remind yourself that miracles are rightfully yours.

Since miracles are always shared, in asking for your rights,
you are upholding the rights of everyone
to know their true Identity.
This is the sweetness of salvation!

Now say, with confidence, "I am entitled to miracles."

Sweet dreams of Awakening

Good Night, Appointed One.

Spend some quiet time with Your Father
before you fall asleep tonight. Ask Him to help you
replace your grievances with the miracles of Love
which are your legacy.

He will appoint many saviors to save you from yourself.
If you accept this mission, you will save your saviors, too,
for in claiming miracles, you shower the whole world
with miracles of grace and healing, starting right now!

Sweet dreams of Awakening

Good Night, Unified Mind.

*It turns out that what seemed to be many problems
boils down to just one: your belief in separation.*

*Now that you recognize this, cuddle up
with Your Father and ask for the solution.
You will find you already have the Answer.*

Sweet dreams of Awakening

Good Night, Carefree Child.

Now it is time to accept the one solution
to the non-problem. This world mesmerizes
with its many dark forms, but
your True Nature is Illuminated Constancy.

Curl up next to Your Father, Who strokes your cheek
and assures you that all your problems have been solved.

Sweet dreams of Awakening

Good Night, Calm Light.

*How holy are You, Who have been given
the function of lighting up the world!*

*Be still before your holiness:
in its calm light let all your conflicts disappear.
In its peace, remember Who You Are.*

Sweet dreams of Awakening

Good Night, Luminous One.

The light of the world brings peace to every mind
through your forgiveness, for your forgiveness is the means
by which the light of the world flows through you
healing the whole world, along with yourself.

Accept this and experience the Joy
that God intends for you this luminous night.

Sweet dreams of Awakening

82

Good Night, Happy Feet.

Your Father is tickled pink when you choose to be happy.
And you get happy feet when you feel Your Father's Joy.

So choose forgiveness and devote yourself to
God's one loving purpose: happiness for One and All.

Sweet dreams of Awakening

Good Night, God's Creation.

Love created you like Itself:
unified, formless, timeless, and loving.

Stop replacing your Creator with idols and self-concepts,
and the Truth becomes obvious.
You are not a body, born to suffer and die.
You are as God created you, eternally Alive and Loving.

Embrace this Reality tonight and know you are Embraced.

Sweet dreams of Awakening

Good Night, Open Mind.

To truly see, you must lay grievances aside.
Join Light and Vision and the entire world is saved!
Salvation has not left its Source,
and so it cannot have left your mind.

Tonight, reach within you and beyond,
and see the Light that shines in us as One.

Sweet dreams of Awakening

Good Night, Child of God.

Lay your head on your pillow and be at peace.
You were mistaken about what and where salvation is.

Stop defeating your own best interests and accept
that only God's plan for salvation will make you happy.

Now, quietly rejoice because His plan can never fail.

Sweet dreams of Awakening

Good Night, Light Being.

It is not your will to grope about in darkness,
fearful of shadows and afraid of things unseen and unreal.

Let Light be your guide tonight:
Follow where Light leads you,
look only on what Light shows you, and
experience the Inner Peace that only Light provides.

Sweet dreams of Awakening

Good Night, Radiant Love.

*The light has come because you **are** the Light.*

You suffer only when you believe in ego laws.
The truth is, you are under no laws but God's.
God's Law is Unified Loving Light,
of which you are the natural extension.

Stop resisting and radiate glorious Love-Light.

Sweet dreams of Awakening

88

Good Night, Miracle Channel.

You are entitled to miracles,
because miracles are your birthright as a Child of God.

Miracles channel the Loving Light which created you,
through you, to your brothers, and back to you.

Relax into this Truth and accept the miracles
which are yours as you sleep tonight.

Sweet dreams of Awakening

Good Night, Unified Mind.

When you give all your problems to the Holy Spirit,
you find out there is just one problem
at the root of them all.

And that one problem is a false belief
that you and your Father have separated.

Come into the present moment,
let your Father love you as you drift to sleep,
and discover that you have been Unified all along.

Sweet dreams of Awakening

Good Night, Miraculous One.

Miracles and Vision go together.
The miracle is always here, although
you cannot see in self-made darkness.

*Denial of Light makes darkness seem real, **but it is not.***
God's Strength is yours as you lift your faith
from body-identity and ask sincerely, "What am I?"

Now, close the body's eyes and open your Spiritual Eye.

Sweet dreams of Awakening

91

Good Night, Abiding Light.

Tonight, leave the dark behind
and enter into the Light of Truth.
Miracles are seen in Light,
and Light and Strength are One.

Enter God's Abode and notice Light
does not shift between night and day.
Light is the Vision with which you truly see.

Eyelids grow heavy, yet keep a steady gaze
upon the Light that glows beyond appearances.

Sweet dreams of Awakening

Good Night, Innocent One.

You are as God created you.

Whatever evil or mistakes you believe were done,
by you or to you, all sinlessness is guaranteed by God.

You and your brothers are, and will forever be,
Your Father's One Son, His Innocent Child.

You dreamt a bad dream, but the Truth remains unchanged:
Light and Joy and Peace abide in you
because God put them there.

Sweet dreams of Awakening

Good Night, True Self.

Let the sights and sounds of this world
be wiped away forever by one idea:

You are as God created you.

Lay aside everything, both bad and good,
and wait, right now, in silent expectancy,
to find out for yourself that
your True Self has never left its Home.

Sweet dreams of Awakening

Good Night, One Self.

You are One Self, united with your Creator,
at one with every aspect of creation, and
limitless in power and in peace.

You are God's Son, One Self, with one goal:
to bring awareness of this Oneness to all minds.

You are complete and healed and whole, One Self,
with full power to use this night to access your Inner Light.

Sweet dreams of Awakening

Good Night, Spirit Self.

Salvation is the memory of God that lives within you.
Each time you choose to remember your True Identity,
you accumulate treasures of Love.

Lay your head on your Father's Chest and say,
"Salvation comes from my One Self."

Relax as the memory of your Spirit Self arises naturally.

Sweet dreams of Awakening

Good Night, One Spirit.

*You are the Spirit in whose mind abides
the miracle in which all time stands still.*

*Devote every minute of sleep tonight to Spirit
and radiate Love around this aching world.
Every open mind and heart will accept
the healing gifts your Light-filled minutes bring.*

*And you will be gifted a thousandfold
and more, as you give and receive
a gleaming chain of interlocking miracles.*

Sweet dreams of Awakening

97

Good Night, Quiet Certainty.

Tonight, be the glad receiver of Your Father's gifts,
that you may share them with the world.

Let Him tenderly kiss your forehead and bless you
as you say, "I accept my part in God's Plan for salvation."

Feel His Word join with yours in quiet certainty,
and accept His gifts of Freedom, Peace and Joy.

Sweet dreams of Awakening

Good Night, Kind Savior.

Salvation reflects Truth in the borderland
between time and Timelessness.

Open your secrets to Your Father's Kindly Light.
Let Him illumine all darkened spots in your mind.

Thus are you saved as all fear is gently laid aside,
and Love claims its rightful place in you.

Sweet dreams of Awakening

Good Night, Happy Face.

If you are sad, your part in salvation is unfulfilled,
and all the world is thus deprived of joy, along with you.

Tonight, and every night, God Smiles on you.
Deliver His Smile to all your sisters and brothers;
your face grows happy as His Joy is reflected back to you.

Sweet dreams of Awakening

Good Night, Perfect Happiness.

Salvation and Atonement do not ask for penance.
There is no price to pay for God's unconditional Love.
God's Will for you is Perfect Happiness.

Joy is just, and pain is but the sign
you have misunderstood yourself.
Sleep tonight with joy in your heart,
now that you are on freedom's road.

Let God's Wings spread through your dreams
with Mighty Magnificence this very eve.

Sweet dreams of Awakening

Good Night, Happy Child.

Your Father is helping you uproot the mistaken identity
that has been occupying your mind.
He wants you to recognize you are free!
Free of pain and suffering, free of sin and despair.

God's Will for you is perfect happiness;
the happiness of Divine Abstract Mind.
Accept you are His Happy Child tonight,
for happiness, forgiveness and salvation are the same.

Sweet dreams of Awakening

Good Night, Joy Heart.

God, being Love, is also Happiness.
Let God's Joy replace your fear and pain.

Tonight, let Your Father stroke your hair
as you drift off to sleep in His Arms.
Listen, as He Says: "You, My Child,
are My Love and Joy."

Sweet dreams of Awakening

103

Good Night, Truth Seeker.

Tonight, a holy place is cleared within your mind, removing all things you thought you wanted, and uncovering God's gifts of Peace and Joy instead.

His are the gifts that you inherited before time was, and that are still yours now. Say with confidence, "I seek but what belongs to me in Truth."

Sweet dreams of Awakening

104

Good Night, Blessed Peace.

Your Father blesses you with Peace and Joy;
He thanks you for accepting His gifts.

In spiritual law, receiving is giving,
so when you accept God's Love,
you share God's Love with every brother far and wide.

Close your eyes a while and tell yourself,
"God's Peace and Joy are mine."

Your Father now assures you this is true.

Sweet dreams of Awakening

105

Good Night, Stillness Itself.

Listen to the Word which lifts the veil
that lies upon the earth, and wakes all those who sleep
and cannot see. God calls to them through you.

He needs your voice to speak to them, for who
could reach God's Son except his Father,
calling through your Self?

Be still and hear Him tonight,
by listening to the simplicity of Truth.

Sweet dreams of Awakening

Good Night, One Truth.

You are not made of flesh and blood and bone,
but are created by the selfsame Thought
which gave the gift of life to Christ as well.

Let God lead you gently to the Truth,
which envelops you in Perfect Peace. Yet,
be glad to return to the world a little while longer,
for Truth will ripple miracles through you
to all your brothers who are One in the Sonship.

Say, "Let truth correct all errors in my mind,
And I will rest in Him Who is my Self."

Sweet dreams of Awakening

107

Good Night, Unified Mind.

Light shines away all conflict and reveals
that to give and to receive are one in Truth.

Light dissolves all paradoxes, letting Oneness prevail.
This night deliver Light instead of darkness:
To everyone, offer quietness.
To everyone, offer peace of mind.
To everyone, offer gentleness.

Now, notice that your mind is healed
for a unified mind must receive all that it gives.

Sweet dreams of Awakening

Good Night, Rested One.

"I rest in God" is a Thought that heals all suffering
and wakens the sleeping Truth in you
and everyone throughout the world.

No more fearful dreams come,
now that you have chosen peace.

Close your eyes, sink into stillness,
and whisper sincerely, "I rest in God."

Sweet dreams of Awakening

Good Night, God's Creation.

You are as God created you.
The healing power of this idea is limitless.
It is the birthplace of all miracles; it is the Truth
that comes to set you free.

Tonight, turn the key that opens
the gate of Heaven and Know your Self
as God created You.

Sweet dreams of Awakening

Good Night, Holy Light.

Miracles are seen in Light.
You cannot see in darkness.
Tonight, let the Light of holiness
and truth illuminate your mind.

See the Innocence within!

Sweet dreams of Awakening

111

Good Night, Abiding One.

You are the home of Light and Joy and Peace.
You are created by the Changeless like Himself.

Your Father is One with you, and you with He.
Accept this now, for you are as He created You.

Sweet dreams of Awakening

Good Night, One Self.

Serenity and Perfect Peace are yours tonight.
You are One Self, completely whole, at one
with all creation and united with your Creator.

Sweet dreams of Awakening

Good Night, Unified Self.

You are the Child of God, resurrected, whole and holy.
Dream this night that you are free of a body,
for you are as God created You.

Your function is to accept the Word of God
and remember the Unified Self you truly are.

Sweet dreams of Awakening

Good Night, Humble Savior.

*Tonight, let Your Father tell you
a bedtime story of how essential you are
in His plan for salvation of the world.*

Forgive and be forgiven.

Sweet dreams of Awakening

Good Night, Happy Love.

Your Father wants nothing more than for you
to awaken to your natural state of Happiness.

His Will is Your Will, when
you recognize What You Really Are.

Tonight, open your mind to His Love,
and find out it is Yours as well.

Sweet dreams of Awakening

Good Night, Love Joy.

Love is your heritage,
and so is joy. These are the gifts
Your Father gives to you.

Entertain no substitutes for Love.
Instead, give your Father joy by
accepting His gifts this very night.

Sweet dreams of Awakening

117

Good Night, Perfect Child.

Tonight, accept God's peace
and joy, in glad exchange for all
the substitutes that you have made.

Let your own feeble voice be still, and
then do you hear the mighty Voice for Truth Itself
assure you that You are God's Perfect Child.

Sweet dreams of Awakening

Good Night, Innocent Self.

*Rest safely in Your Father's Mind tonight
and learn to recognize your Innocence.*

*Forgive all people, places and things,
and discover your free and innocent Self.*

Sweet dreams of Awakening

Good Night, Perfect Certainty.

Rest deeply in God this very night and
He will work in you and through you.

Rest completely in Him, and
in quiet and perfect certainty
you will hear Him tell you What You Really Are.

Sweet dreams of Awakening

Good Night, Perfect Happiness.

Forgiveness is the key to happiness.
Tonight, awaken from the dream
that you are mortal, fallible and full of sin.

Know, instead, that you are the perfect Child of God.

Sweet dreams of Awakening

121

Good Night, Sparkling Joy.

Do you want happiness, a quiet mind,
a certainty of purpose, and a sense of worth
and beauty that transcends the world?

Forgiveness sparkles within you when you accept salvation,
which stands before you like an open door,
with warmth and welcome, bidding you enter
and make yourself at Home, where you belong,
once you forgive and realize you are forgiven.

Tonight, walk directly into the Light
and feel the Joy the lifting of the veil holds out to you.

Sweet dreams of Awakening

Good Night, Lightened Footstep.

*Tonight, receive God's Thanks to you
and feel how lovingly He holds you in His Mind.*

*His care for you is deep and limitless;
His gratitude to you is immense!*

*He saves you from the self you thought you made
and shines away all resistance to His gifts.*

*Devote your slumber to giving thanks and
in the morning walk with lightened footsteps,
smiling upon everyone you see.*

Sweet dreams of Awakening

Good Night, Holy Mind.

You are One with God.

Tonight, notice it is effortless to join your mind
with the Loving and the Lovable because
your God-Mind contains only Loving Thoughts.

As you accept that Your Father overflows with Love
for you and your brothers, you are transfigured.
Receive His gift of Holy Peace right now.

Sweet dreams of Awakening

124

Good Night, God's Word.

Your Father calls to you from deep
within your mind where He abides.

He speaks from nearer than your heart;
His Voice is closer than your hand.
His Word is yours.

Listen quietly and receive His Truth in stillness:
underlying all mad illusions, you and your brothers
are wholly joined in holy Peace and Love.

Sweet dreams of Awakening

125

Good Night, Quiet Savior.

Give Your Father your faith tonight.
Accept the Help He offers you.

In silence, close your eyes upon the world
that does not understand forgiveness, and
seek sanctuary in the quiet place
where thoughts are healed
and false beliefs laid by.

All that you give is given to your Self;
open your mind to Understand.

Sweet dreams of Awakening

Good Night, Love of God.

Love is a law without an opposite,
limitless and all-inclusive.
Love is what You are, the link between
Your Father and Your Self.

Tonight, call to Him Who has promised to Answer.
Ask Him to light the spark of Truth
within your clean and open mind.

Sweet dreams of Awakening

127

Good Night, Worthy Self.

The world you see holds nothing that you want.
Tonight, escape the chains you placed upon your own mind.

Let go of the prison bars you constructed and
instantly you rise above the world, flying
with holy purpose to rest in your Creator.

Be restored to sanity, to freedom and to Love.
Your Guide is sure; open your mind to Him and rest.

Sweet dreams of Awakening

Good Night, Heaven's Grace.

Tonight the lights of Heaven bend to you,
to shine upon your eyelids as you rest
beyond the world of darkness.

Here is Light your eyes cannot behold.
And yet your mind can see it plainly, and Understands.

Beyond the earthly world there is a world you want.
Let grace guide you there.

Sweet dreams of Awakening

Good Night, Unified Love.

Empty your hands, with thanks and faith,
of all the earthly treasures you hold dear.
Their value is false.

Ask for a strength beyond your own
to deliver you from temptation.

Accept God's strength,
and freedom and deliverance
are both yours and your brother's
this blessed night.

Sweet dreams of Awakening

130

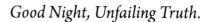

Good Night, Unfailing Truth.

Why wait for Heaven when It is here now?
Time is the great illusion of past and future
which inevitably concludes in death.

Happily, these are foolish imaginings!
And no one can fail who seeks to reach the Truth.
So ask Your Father to show you
the unfailing Truth of unchanging Love
and you shall receive His Vision.

Be glad! Angels light the way to the
Heavenly Home you have never left.

Sweet dreams of Awakening

131

Good Night, Free Thinker.

It may seem like your thoughts are out of control,
but truly it is the opposite. Release your mind and
your Inner Spirit will show you a free and beautiful world!

Let the Free Thinker in you help you realize
you are as God created you, for ideas leave not their Source.
When you loose the world from what you thought it was,
you free yourself and your brothers, inside and out.

Here is the joyous discovery that
you are where you have always been,
safe and snug at Home in Heaven.

Sweet dreams of Awakening

Good Night, Shining Halo.

Heaven Itself is reached with empty hands and open minds,
which come with nothing to find everything
and claim it as their own.

This eve, come to Your Father with
honest willingness to value only what is valuable.
Then receive what waits for everyone who reaches,
unencumbered, the gate of Heaven,
which swings wide open in welcome.

Sweet dreams of Awakening

133

Good Night, True Forgiveness.

Daytime is but a waking dream,
and nighttime brings sleeping dreams.
Both keep you in chains until you find
the door to true forgiveness, which frees you
and your brothers from sinful and punishing illusions.

Tonight, follow the Guide God gave you and
cross the bridge from ego hell to Heaven's gate.
Let your step be light, and as you walk
stars sparkle in your wake, pointing
the way to all who follow you.

Sweet dreams of Awakening

Good Night, Defenseless Strength.

*What could you not accept, if you but knew
that everything that happens, past, present and future,
is gently planned by One Whose only purpose is your good?
All your defenses have denied His blessings, but
God's benedictions remain Shining behind your blockade.*

*Your slumber tonight contains the holy instant,
set in time, but heeding only Immortality.
Ask that your body be used for Love, not fear.
Then receive the Light which proves that you
need no defense against the truth of your Reality.*

Sweet dreams of Awakening

Good Night, Healthy Spirit.

Healing flashes across the open mind
that is no longer interested in
quick forgetting and self-deception.

Body health is not the measurement of a healthy Spirit.
Accept that sickness is a defense against the Truth
and Peace and Wholeness arise, in place of false identity.

Say, "I have forgotten What I really am,
for I mistook my body for my Self.
But I am not a body, so I cannot be sick.
I will accept the truth of What I am, and
let my mind be wholly healed tonight."

Sweet dreams of Awakening

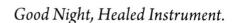

Good Night, Healed Instrument.

Those who are healed become the instruments of healing.
Nor does time elapse between the instant you are healed,
and all the grace of healing it is given you to give.

Say, "I would share my healing with the world,
that sickness may be banished from the mind
of God's One Child, Who is my only Self.

Sweet dreams of Awakening

137

Good Night, Conscious Choice.

Heaven is already in your Mind.
All that is veiled in shadows
must be raised to Understanding.

Consciously choose Heaven and
the shield of unawareness with which
the ego has disguised its pseudo-being
is shown to be flimsy and transparent in the Light.

Tonight, make the choice for Truth and know
Your Father's Mighty Magnificence is your own.

Sweet dreams of Awakening

138

Good Night, Holy Mind.

You have a holy mission here.
It is to accept the Atonement
so you can offer it to your brothers.

Atonement unlocks the final link in the chain
with which you unknowingly imprisoned yourself.
Now, you are undone, pure and Free!

Tonight, embrace the Truth
by repeating as you fall asleep:
"I accept Atonement for myself,
for I remain as God created me."

Sweet dreams of Awakening

139

Good Night, Salvation's Cure.

True healing is of the Mind.
Come with lifted heart and listening mind
to feel salvation cover you with soft protection,
and peace so deep that no illusion can disturb you.

Tonight, Your Father sends you happy dreams
as heralds of the dawn of Truth upon your mind.
And thus salvation cures ego amnesia
and You remember Who you really are.

Sweet dreams of Awakening

Good Night, Timeless One.

Your mind holds only what you think with God.

There is no hurry, for tonight
you are using time for His Timeless purpose.
Forgiveness is the key to happiness
because it reveals the past is over.

Forgiveness offers everything you want
for it is the great release from time.

Sweet dreams of Awakening

Good Night, Clean Slate.

Tonight, clear your mind of all thoughts
that would deceive by saying,
"My mind holds only what I think with God."

Ask Your Father for His gifts to you;
and thank Him for His unconditional Love
which envelops you in the Oneness you already are.

Sweet dreams of Awakening

Good Night, Complete Communion.

Your mind holds only what you think with God.
In quiet receive God's Word tonight.
It tells you all are One.

Therefore, all that you give
is given to your One Self.
Commune with Your Lord
and receive Completion.

Sweet dreams of Awakening

Good Night, Endless Quiet.

There is no Love but God's.
The world you see holds nothing that you want.

But happily, your mind holds only what you think with God.
Choose to be enveloped by this Endless Quiet
and find out Who You Are and Who Your Father Is.

Sweet dreams of Awakening

Good Night, Heaven's Gate.

Beyond this world there is a world you want.
Follow the Steadily Shining Light in your mind
and you will reach Heaven's Gate tonight.

There it becomes clear that in Truth,
it is impossible to see two worlds.

Now, unhurriedly enter the Home you never left
aware that your mind holds only what you think with God.

Sweet dreams of Awakening

Good Night, Total Success.

No one can fail who seeks to reach the Truth.
It is inevitable that all will awaken, eventually.
The sooner you release the world
from all you thought it was,
the sooner you discover that your mind
holds only what you think with God.

Sweet dreams of Awakening

146

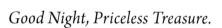

Good Night, Priceless Treasure.

When you perceive forgiveness as it is,
you will no longer value what is valueless.

Forgiveness restores your communion with God's Mind
in which there is never loss and always gain.

Accept His Message and rest in perfect certainty
that your mind overflows with all that is Valuable
because your mind holds only what you think with God.

Sweet dreams of Awakening

147

Good Night, Holy Harmony.

If you defend yourself, you bear witness
to the idea that you have been attacked.

But since your mind holds only what you think
with God, Holy Harmony cannot attack Itself.

Sickness and conflict are the same;
both are defenses against the Truth,
but You do not need defenses anymore.

Sweet dreams of Awakening

148

Good Night, One Mind.

When you are healed, all are healed with you.
*They may not know it, but **you do** because*
as you realize your mind holds only
what you think with God
you also recognize all is One.

Tonight, decide for Heaven and feel God offer thanks
to You Who accept His inheritance as One Self.

Sweet dreams of Awakening

149

Good Night, Unobscured Illumination.

Your self-deceptions cannot take the place of Reality.
Only lack of forgiveness blocks the Light of Truth.

Your mind holds only what you think with God.
Accept Atonement and receive salvation's cure
which removes all obstacles and restores Illumination.

Sweet dreams of Awakening

Good Night, Purified Thought.

Hear God whisper in your ear, Wordlessly
assuring you that all things are echoes of His Voice.

Give Him your thoughts that He may remove
the elements of dreams and give them back again
as clean ideas that contradict not His Will.

Your Life exists beyond the body and the world.
Let your mind be purified by your Creator tonight,
and your thoughts transformed into joyous miracles.

Sweet dreams of Awakening

Good Night, Co-Creator.

It is time to take your rightful place
as co-creator of the Universe.

Humbly ask to have your True Self revealed to you.
Say, "The power of decision is my own.
Tonight I accept myself as what
my Father's Will created me to be."

Now be silent and let He Who never left
blossom blissfully into your awareness.

Sweet dreams of Awakening

Good Night, Invulnerable Child.

*Defensiveness is weakness, yet defenselessness is Strength;
this paradox contains the key to your Invulnerable Identity.*

*Look past worldly dreams tonight;
instead, be still, and in silence rest securely in God's Love,
untouchable within His Light. Salvation was designed by
Your Father to teach you that the game of fear is gone.*

*Sleep safely and serenely with faith that
there is nothing you need defend against.*

Sweet dreams of Awakening

153

Good Night, God's Minister.

Would you receive the messages of God?
Just ask and the Message will be given.
Then share His Message as your intuition guides you,
for giving is receiving and in this way
both you and your brother are blessed.

The world recedes as you let God illuminate your mind.

Sweet dreams of Awakening

Good Night, God's Completion.

*Your feet are safely set
upon the road that leads to God.*

*He has placed His Hand in yours.
Step back in faith and feel your forehead
grow serene, your eyes quiet, as you grasp His Hand.*

*Your Father speaks of His Limitless Love for you
and how His Name is Your Own. Let Him guide you Home.*

Sweet dreams of Awakening

155

Good Night, Perfect Holiness.

There is a Light in you which cannot die;
this Light is what your brothers yearn to behold.
The Light you emanate is reflected back to you.

Ask tonight, "Who walks with me?"
and hear God's Answer as you say,
"I walk with God in perfect holiness.
I light the world, I light my mind,
and all minds which God created One with me."

Sweet dreams of Awakening

156

Good Night, Child of God.

Into Christ's Presence do you enter now,
serenely unaware of everything except
His Shining Face and Perfect Love.

Tonight, the Holy Giver of Happy Dreams
uses your sleep to give you a touch of Heaven.

Sweet dreams of Awakening

Good Night, Giving Receiver.

Time is a vast illusion in which
there is no single instant when the body exists at all.

Forget your body and enter Your Mind.
Here is a quiet place made holy by forgiveness and by Love.

You attain Christ's Vision when you give as you receive.
The script is written; all stories are told.
Tonight, see no one as a body, with history,
but greet all as a Child of God,
acknowledging One Spirit Self.

Sweet dreams of Awakening

158

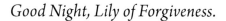

Good Night, Lily of Forgiveness.

All miracles are given you to give your brothers
in order to receive the very miracle
you thought you gave away.

Christ's treasure can only increase through giving.
Christ-Mind has dreamed a dream of
a forgiven world fragrant with lilies.
Breathe in this exquisite aroma of Love,
and dream with Christ, for You are He.

Sweet dreams of Awakening

159

Good Night, Fearless Love.

Whom God has joined remains forever One,
at home in Him, no stranger to your Self.

Fear is the stranger when you accept God's Vision
and behold all your brothers as One Self, joyously United.
Not one does Christ forget, so let us
snuggle up together safe at Home.

Sweet dreams of Awakening

Good Night, Blessed Child.

Each night, Your Father sings you
an ancient melody you forgot but know so well:
Complete abstraction is the natural condition of the mind.
This Knowledge is your safe escape from anger and fear.

You are not forgot in Heaven. To remember this,
bless anybody who has upset you, and call him brother,
for this choice reveals the holy Innocence you both share.

Sweet dreams of Awakening

161

Good Night, God's Creation.

You are as God created you.
These sacred words dispel the night,
and darkness is no more.

Keep "I am as God created me,"
in your mind as you fall asleep,
when you arise, and all day long!

You are as God created you.
Holy indeed are you who make these words your own.

Sweet dreams of Awakening

Good Night, Eternal Life.

Relax into God's Embrace and accept there is no death.
How could the Source of Life contain Its own demise?

See beyond insane ego beliefs and look upon the glorious
reflection of Your Love which shines in everything.

Align your thoughts and will with
Your Father's and know all Beings as Eternal.

Sweet dreams of Awakening

163

Good Night, Ancient Melody.

Tonight, leave a clean and open space
within your mind to receive the treasure of salvation.

God kisses your forehead and Vision from
far beyond this world imbues everything with His Light.
All seeming sins are forgot; all sorrow unremembered
for now are You One with Him Who is Your Source.

Hear the ancient melody of Silence
which is always in your heart.
Listen to the Song of Heaven softly croon you Home.

Sweet dreams of Awakening

Good Night, Heavenly Child.

*Lay aside denial and accept the Thought of God
as your rightful inheritance. Hesitate no longer!
Count on God, not yourself, and
Heaven is yours for the asking.*

*Ask to receive and the Thought of God protects you,
cares for you, makes soft your resting place and smooth
your way, lighting your mind with Happiness and Love.*

Sweet dreams of Awakening

165

Good Night, Gifted One.

Tonight, become aware of Christ's gentle touch
upon your shoulder; there is no need to feel alone.
Your Companion is Your Self; God's Child is
One Unified Identity gifting Love to Itself.

God has entrusted all His gifts to You.
Now share them with your brothers
that you may know their Joy.

Sweet dreams of Awakening

166

Good Night, Awake Mind.

A sleeping mind must waken,
as it sees its own Perfection mirroring
the Lord of Life so perfectly it fades into
what is reflected there. The ego calls this death,
but it is actually the end of all bad dreams.

Your Father does not sleep nor die and neither can You.
There is only One Life, and that You share with God.
Close your eyes and discover Your Awake Mind
which is One with its Source, its Self, its Holiness.

Sweet dreams of Awakening

167

Good Night, Never-Changing Love.

Tonight, God comes Himself to sweep away
the cobwebs of your sleep. His gift of grace
restores all memories of Love the sleeping mind forgot.

The memory of Him awakens in the mind
that asks the means of Him whereby its sleep is done!
Simply say, "Your grace is given me. I claim it now.
Father, I come to You. And You come to me who ask.
For I am the Child You love."

Sweet dreams of Awakening

Good Night, God's Grace.

*Tonight release all thoughts of "you"
so that your mind is a clean altar
ready to receive God's gift of grace.*

*Grace is the acceptance of the Love of God,
which enters into an open mind and heart.
Ask for grace, and welcome the release
grace offers everyone as it pours through you
in a healing stream of holy instants.*

Sweet dreams of Awakening

Good Night, Heart of Love.

Fear makes way for courage when you
discover your inner Heart of Love.
Now you can face the terrible unholy instant
when you forgot your Source.

Tonight, undo the mistakes of ego mind by praying,
"Father, I am like You, so no cruelty abides in me.
Your Peace and Love are mine. And I bless this world
with what I have received from You. I choose again,
and make my choice for all my brothers, knowing they
are one with Us. Holy are We because Your Holiness
has set Us free. And We give thanks. Alleluia!"

Sweet dreams of Awakening

170

Good Night, Divine Meaning.

Use words to go beyond words
to the divine meaning within.

Let God's Love echo through your mind
as you sleep tonight and know
the power of decision is your own.
Decide now:
"God is but Love, and therefore so am I."

Sweet dreams of Awakening

171

Good Night, Minister of God.

All are invited into God's Ministry;
everyone is equal here. And here you find
that in your defenselessness your safety lies.
No competition; no more attacks and defenses.

Tonight, rather than mindlessly counting sheep,
repeat this until supreme mantra as you fall asleep,
"God is but Love, and therefore so am I."

Sweet dreams of Awakening

Good Night, Perfect Holiness.

God loves you and you are His Love.
It is time to step back and let Him lead the way.
Walk with Your Father on a journey without distance
to a place you have never left, for He is your Source
and your Source is Perfect Holiness.

Remember, God is but Love,
and therefore so are You.

Sweet dreams of Awakening

Good Night, One Presence.

Let God tuck you in and accept His tender kiss
on your forehead, and each precious eyelid
to open your spiritual Eye and enter fully
into His Singular Presence tonight.

Learn that He is your Creator and you share One Self,
for union has no dividing lines. In this way, it is Seen
that giving and receiving are the same.
In this way, it is Known that God is but Love,
and therefore so are You.

Sweet dreams of Awakening

Good Night, Same Name.

It is most natural to inherit the family Name.
Though you dreamt of exile, you are still at Home,
safe and snug with Your Father.
There can be no fear in Heaven.

This very night,
accept the miracles you have been given
and give the miracles you have received.
After all, God is but Love, and therefore so are You.

Sweet dreams of Awakening

175

Good Night, God's Creation.

God showers you with blessings as you drift to sleep.
You are, and always will be, as He created you:
Innocent, Beautiful and Free.

Step by step, walk the path of Light He shines before you,
and know that God is but Love, and therefore so are You.

Sweet dreams of Awakening

Good Night, God-Child.

If you only knew how sweet and tender
God's Love for you is, your heart would melt
and you would overflow with love
for everyone and everything everywhere!

Every day and every night you would know that Life
cannot contain death and you would be free of all fear.

As it sinks in that you are One
with Him Who is Your Source you will know,
"God is but Love, and therefore so am I."

Sweet dreams of Awakening

Good Night, Complete Union.

Let not your mind deny the Thought of God
with Whom you share complete union.
Indeed, He has entrusted you with His gifts.
The Truth is, you Complete each other.

Accept the lullaby He softly sings, "I am but Love,
and therefore so are You, Infinite, Sweet and True.
I am but Love, and therefore so are You."

Sweet dreams of Awakening

178

Good Night, One Life.

*There is only One Life
and you share this Life with God.
He gives you His grace
and when you choose to claim it
you discover that God is but Love,
and therefore so are You.*

Sweet dreams of Awakening

Good Night, Gracious Love.

By grace you live. By grace you are released.
In doing so, you prove to yourself
there is no meanness in God and, at your essence,
none in you or your brothers. How could there be?
For your Source is but Love, and therefore so are You.

Accept His Love and be lit from within as you slumber.
Tomorrow, you will shine this Mighty Love into the world.

Sweet dreams of Awakening

Good Night, Holy Self.

As you lay your head on your pillow,
look neither ahead or backwards,
but straight into the Present and
give your trust to the holy Self
which is your true Identity.

If a sin, your brother's or your own, occurs to you, say:
"It is not this that I would look upon.
I trust my brothers, who are One with me."

Then, rest as God rocks you in His Arms,
assuring you this is no fantasy; you, your brothers,
and Your Father are, indeed, One sinless Self.

Sweet dreams of Awakening

181

Good Night, Holy Child.

There is a Child in you Who seeks His Father's house,
and knows that He is alien here. This Child abides in you
and you in Him. He whispers of His Home unceasingly.

Be still an instant and your Innocence is restored.
Lay down your sword and find that you are Protected.
You have not lost your Innocence and it shall not be denied.
Be still an instant and go Home with Him.

Sweet dreams of Awakening

Good Night, God's Name.

Say Your Name with conviction
as you fall asleep tonight:
"I am as God created me!"

Watch as angels surround your bed and
spread their wings to shelter you from
every worldly thought intruding upon your Holiness.

Hear them sing a song of Oneness.
You have acknowledged Your Father as the
sole Creator of Reality and thus are you released!

Sweet dreams of Awakening

Good Night, One Name.

The Name of God is Your inheritance.
Stop settling for names and labels you have dreamed up.
Feel your Spirit Eye open
as Your Father kisses your forehead.

True vision unifies the mind!
Every gap closes and all separation is healed.
Be glad that you can melt into the Un-Nameable
as One Name disappears into the nirvana of Oneness.

Sweet dreams of Awakening

184

Good Night, Peace of God.

*No one who truly seeks the Peace of God
can fail to find it. Ask, with deep sincerity,
to deceive yourself no more and Quiet Arises.
Here, you are nothing but the Peace of God.*

*Allow that Fact to sparkle in your mind
and electrify your sleep with God's Light.*

Sweet dreams of Awakening

185

Good Night, Humble Love.

God 's gentle Voice calls to you all night long,
whispering Truth and Knowledge into your trusting ear.

You hear Him because deep inside you recognize
His Message and you desire nothing
but to receive the Love He gives.

This Love is as Great as it is Humble
and you are transformed by the purity of Truth.

Sweet dreams of Awakening

186

Good Night, Blessed One.

Let the Wordless Name of God echo
through your mind as you sleep tonight.
See the purity of Heaven shining the reflection
of your Holy Self mirrored back to you.

The grace of God shines in everyone.
Behold His lilies and your own blessed Innocence.

Sweet dreams of Awakening

187

Good Night, Heavenly Light.

Tonight, accept God's help in excluding the outer world,
and let your thoughts fly to His Peace within you.

Accept His Word as you sleep, and dark fantasies
and shadows melt away, revealing your Heavenly Light,
for enlightenment is but a recognition, not a change at all.

The luminous peace of God is shining in you now.

Sweet dreams of Awakening

Good Night, Love of God.

Be still and lay aside all thoughts
of what you are and what God is.

Empty your mind of everything it thinks
is true or false, good or bad, right or wrong.

Forget this world and come with wholly empty hands
unto your Source. In your quiet heart and open mind,
God's Love blazes a pathway Home.

Sweet dreams of Awakening

189

Good Night, Holy Joy.

Lay down the ruthless sword of judgment
you have been holding against your throat.
This is the night to realize that all guilt is illusion.

Reality is Joy. Pain is deception; Joy alone is Truth.
Anguish is but sleep and Joy never sleeps.
Look deep and See your Holy Mind can only hold pure Joy.

Sweet dreams of Awakening

190

Good Night, Child of God.

Be glad tonight how easily hell is undone.
You who perceive yourself as weak and frail,
with futile hopes and devastated dreams hear this:
All power is given unto you in earth and Heaven.

There is nothing that you cannot do,
for miracles light up dark and ancient caverns
if you but ask for them.

Child of God, ***ask now,*** *and discover*
You are Glorious, Whole and Free!

Sweet dreams of Awakening

191

Good Night, Formless Self.

Forgiveness is your function while you walk the earth.
Forgiveness gently leaves the world
a clean and unmarked slate on which the Word of God
replaces guilt, punishment, fear and death.

Only forgiveness can relieve the mind of thinking
that the body is its home. Hold no one prisoner.
You and your brother are as God created you,
Formless, Innocent, and Joined in Joy.

Sweet dreams of Awakening

192

Good Night, Boundless Love.

Tonight, forgive and you will see life differently,
limitless in scope and overflowing with loving kindness.

Lay you down to sleep,
with chains of time released, and
let your mind unwind, unbound,
to the Land of Eternal Peace.

Sweet dreams of Awakening

Good Night, Holy Instant.

This eve, place your future in the Hands of God.
Be gently reassured that doing so replaces
all fear and loss with His Timeless Treasures.

Your foot has reached the lawns
that welcome you to Heaven's gate;
the quiet place of Peace, where you await
with certainty the final step of God,
Who lovingly lifts you up to Him.

Sweet dreams of Awakening

Good Night, Love Walker.

Lay your tired head in God's lap and
let an ancient door within your mind swing open.

Hear, from within,
a long forgotten Word echo in your memory.
This Wordless Word calls you Home,
for Love is the way you walk in gratitude.

Sweet dreams of Awakening

195

Good Night, Sweet Redemption.

Tonight, with your willingness,
the Light of resurrection shines within your Mind.
It takes but a holy instant to recognize
when you join with the grace of God.

Give welcome to this sweet redemption
for the Heart of God overflows with Love for you.

Sweet dreams of Awakening

Good Night, Heart of God.

Your Being in Your Father is secure,
because your will is One with His and
all your brothers, Who are His Child, too.

In your heart the Heart of God is laid.
Give thanks to Your Father and
accept His Thanks to You!

Immerse yourself in His Gratitude tonight
and uncover the Light of Perfection within.

Sweet dreams of Awakening

197

Good Night, Blessed Self.

Forgiveness sweeps all other dreams away,
and though it is itself a dream, it breeds no others.

Forgiveness is a dream in which the Son of God awakens
to his Still Self and Loving Father, knowing They are One.
The time has come to see the face of Christ unveiled.

Sweet dreams of Awakening

Good Night, Ineffable Spirit.

Tonight, take your body off
along with your clothes!
Rest in God, for you are not a body.
You are free.

Cherish the idea that you and your brothers
are Immortality Itself. Declare your
Innocence and know that you are Free!

Accept God's blessing and feel the joy dance within you as
the purpose of the body switches from fear to forgiveness.

Sweet dreams of Awakening

199

Good Night, Peace Child.

There is no peace except the Peace of God.
Be glad and thankful it is so.
Heaven lies before you, through a door that opens easily,
if you but ask for what you already have.

Feel His Peace softly enveloping your heart and mind
with comfort and with love. Settle into your natural
environment and make yourself at Home.

Sweet dreams of Awakening

200

Good Night, Bodiless Freedom.

As you drift to sleep,
sink inwards and contemplate this:
You are One with the Universe,
the Creation of the One Creator
of the Whole which is your Self.

You are not a body. You are free.
For you are still as God created you.

Sweet dreams of Awakening

201

Good Night, Timeless One.

Do not remain an instant more
where you do not belong.
Just be willing to follow
Your Father Home.

Say, "Father, tonight I follow You Home.
For I am not a body. I am free.
Yes, I am still as You created me."

Sweet dreams of Awakening

Good Night, God's Name.

*The Name of God is your deliverance
from every thought of evil and of sin,
because the Name of Love is your legacy.*

*Accept your Real Name by saying,
"I am not a body. I am free.
For I am still as God created me.
And I share His Name for
It belongs to One and All."*

Sweet dreams of Awakening

Good Night, Holy Name.

God's Name is Yours. Tonight, accept this
Living inheritance from Your Timeless Father.
Choose to know you are forever One with
Him Who gives you Peace Eternal
by basking in Formless Love as you rest.

You are not a body. You are free.
For you are still as God created you.

Sweet dreams of Awakening

Good Night, Peaceful One.

The Peace of God is your purpose,
your function and your life,
until you realize you are Home.

Let Peace envelop you tonight,
for you are not a body. You are free.
You are still as God created you.

Sweet dreams of Awakening

Good Night, God's Gift.

Salvation of the world depends on you.
Forgive with the Holy Spirit's Help and
you become your brother's savior as
God's gifts of Love, Peace and Joy
sparkle through you and from you.

You are not a body. You are free.
For you are still as He created you.

Sweet dreams of Awakening

Good Night, Blessed One.

Let all your sorrows melt away as
you accept God's boundless Love for you.
His blessings light your way and
shine within your holy heart,
where He abides always.

To remember this, simply say:
I am not a body. I am free.
For I am still as God created me.

Sweet dreams of Awakening

Good Night, Shining One.

Lay down and be still.
Let all the earth be still along with you.
In this stillness is the peace of God.
It is within your heart and witnesses to God Himself.

Pray: "I am not a body. I am free.
For I am still as God created me."

Sweet dreams of Awakening

Good Night, Loved One.

God created you and God tucks you in tonight.
His Love for you is so vast and tender that
if you let yourself feel it for one moment
you will change your mind forever.

Let the boundless Love of God unchain you.
Say: I am not a body. I am free.
For I am still as My Father created me.

Sweet dreams of Awakening

209

Good Night, Joyful One.

Pain is your own idea. It is not a Thought of God.
Choose God's Will and stop blocking the Joy
which is your True Nature.

Feel Your Father's Smile warming you with Love.
He takes pleasure in His Child, so take pleasure in Him.

Melt into His Truth:
You are not a body. You are free.
For you are still as God created you.

Sweet dreams of Awakening

Good Night, Glorious Love.

Let God cradle you in His Arms and rock you in His Lap.
Listen as He softly croons, "You are not a body.
You are free. For you are still as I created You."

Slumber in silence and true humility
as you accept His Glorious Love.

Sweet dreams of Awakening

211

Good Night, Freedom Rider.

Your Father strokes the hair off your forehead
and gazes at you tenderly as you sleep.

Let Him help you leave illusions behind
and use your dreams to re-establish
the Truth of Who You Are.

You are not a body. You are free.
For you are still as God created you.

Sweet dreams of Awakening

212

Good Night, Miracle Worker.

Let God teach you His Lessons of Love
by giving Him all your pain and shame.
In this way, open as a clear conduit to His Grace
and watch miracles blossom within you!

For you are not a body. You are free.
You are still as God created you.

Sweet dreams of Awakening

213

Good Night, Timeless Presence.

Place the future in the Hands of God
and you are freed from both past and future.
Accept what God gives and receive Knowledge
of the Timeless Presence you already are.

For you are not a body. You are free!
You are still as God created you.

Sweet dreams of Awakening

Good Night, Love Walker.

Humans are sleep walkers both day and night,
for that kind of waking is still a form of dreaming.
But you are not human; you are Being.

Elect to follow the Holy Spirit's guidance
and it becomes impossible to forget:
You are not a body. You are free.
For you are still as God created you.

Sweet dreams of Awakening

215

Good Night, Ascended One.

The message of the crucifixion is perfectly clear:
Teach only Love, for that is what you are.

Resurrection is obvious when you realize:
You are not a body. You are free.
For you are still as God created you!

Sweet dreams of Awakening

Good Night, Great One.

Gratitude acknowledges Greatness.
God continuously gives thanks that you are His Own,
for He is greatly pleased in you, His Creation.

As you accept God's thanks, salvation is yours.
And you become your brothers' savior
for then you confirm for all:

You are not a body. You are free.
For you are still as God created you.

Sweet dreams of Awakening

217

Good Night, Vision of Glory.

Behold God's Glory and be glad, for it is yours as well.

You are not a body. You are free.
For you are still as God created you:
Formless Spirit, Timeless Life,
Luminous with Love and Light.

Sweet dreams of Awakening

Good Night, Quiet Mind.

You are Your Father's Son and
He would have your mind be still.

Rest in His Loving Arms tonight.

In the morning, arise radiant with His Love,
confident that you are not a body, you are free.
For you are still as God created you.

Sweet dreams of Awakening

Good Night, Peace of God.

Sink deeply into Your Father's Arms
as you fall asleep tonight.

Peace is certain when you follow Him
Who leads you Home by saying:
I am not a body. I am free.
For I am still as God created me.

Sweet dreams of Awakening

Good Night, Silent Mind.

Now do we wait in quiet.
God is here, and He will surely
speak with you, and you will hear.

Be confident, for His Voice is the Stillness
within the deep recesses of your heart and mind.
Tonight He speaks of What You Are,
and reveals the Father and the Son are One.

Sweet dreams of Awakening

Good Night, Son Shine.

God is with you. He shines Love upon you,
who also shine Love upon Him. He is the Source of Life;
the Spirit which covers you with kindness and blessings.

Receive His Benediction now by saying:
"Father, I have no words except Your Name
upon my lips and in my mind, as I come quietly
into Your Presence now, and ask to rest
with You in peace forevermore."

Sweet dreams of Awakening

222

Good Night, Timeless Life.

God is your Life; you have no Life but His.
You are Spirit, not a body, and
you share Timeless Life with Him.

It is lonely to believe you are a person,
separate and far from Home.

Claim your Heavenly Name tonight.
Acknowledge you are One with Your Father.

Sweet dreams of Awakening

Good Night, God's Name.

Your true Identity is so secure, so lofty, innocent,
glorious and great, wholly beneficent and free from guilt,
that Heaven looks to It to give It Light.

This Nameless Family Name lights the world as well.
It is the gift Your Father gave to you to give your brothers.
This giving is mutual salvation; it is illusion's end ...
revealed tonight!

Sweet dreams of Awakening

Good Night, Blazing Love.

God's Love bursts and sparkles Infinitely.
He gives all His Love to you, and
you return that Love effortlessly,
for giving and receiving are the same.

The way is open.
Tonight, take Your Father's Hand
and blaze a loving trail on a journey
without distance to a Home you never left.

Sweet dreams of Awakening

Good Night, Homeward Bound.

Your Father's Arms are open wide to embrace you.
His Loving Voice calls you to gladly return Home.
Death is not necessary for this reunion.
All that is required is a change of mind.

Stop seeing value in the false and Light Shines through you,
from beyond you, so that All are Homeward Bound.

Sweet dreams of Awakening

Good Night, Right Mind.

It is time to undress your mind of all ego illusions
and lay them at Your Father's Lotus Feet.
Climb into His Lap, clad in holiness, and listen
as He tells you that your will is One with His.

Lay down bad dreams and
let your Right Mind be restored to you at last
for now is your holy instant of release!

Sweet dreams of Awakening

227

Good Night, God's Word.

You are a luminous extension
of Your Father's Timeless Mind.
God's Creation is Life Itself,
and Life has no opposite.

Take God's Word for Who you truly are
and fully rest in Him. His Word leaves you speechless
with profound peace and boundless joy as It undoes
mistaken identity and dark ego dreams.
Relax and be absorbed in Him.

Sweet dreams of Awakening

Good Night, Face of Love.

*Be willing to see the holy Face of Love in every face,
including your own, and see that Love prevails, always.*

*Your Father clasps Your Face in His Hands
and sees only One Self, innocent and pure.*

*Thank Him, as you fall asleep, for His Perfect Vision.
Say, "Love, which created me, is what I am."*

Sweet dreams of Awakening

Good Night, Undeniable Peace.

In peace you were created.
And in peace do you remain.

Simply ask Your Father what you truly are
and peacefully He rocks you in His Arms
until you stop denying what is True.

Sweet dreams of Awakening

Good Night, Holy Remembrance.

The Thought of Peace has never left you,
though it seems to be forgotten.

Just call on Your Father and Eternity
shines away the world you think is real,
activating the memory of the Home you never left.

Trust that all is given and nothing is taken away, and
free fall into the holy remembrance of what you truly are.

Sweet dreams of Awakening

231

Good Night, Mindful One.

Evening is here and it is time you know
that there is not one minute you dwell without God.

Now, let all your thoughts overflow with His Love.
Your Father would have you sleep sure of your safety,
certain of His care, and happily aware you are His Child.

Sweet dreams of Awakening

Good Night, Wise Follower.

*Tonight, jump into Your Father's Arms
without reserve and question not His Love,
strong and tender beyond comprehension.*

*Receive His Loving Intelligence by
giving Him all your personal thoughts.
Then feel your Self, Empty and Free, as the
mighty Wisdom of the Infinite flows through thee.*

Sweet dreams of Awakening

233

Good Night, Continuous Thought.

God's Thought is forever unified as One,
in which you are included. A tiny, mad instant
elapsed between Eternity and Timelessness
during which you believed you were separate.

Happily, you remain Continuous and Unchanging
as God's cherished Child, along with all your brothers.
Accept this as wholly true tonight and rest easy.

Sweet dreams of Awakening

234

Good Night, Happy Love.

Your Father's Will for you is only happiness.
As you fall asleep tonight, give Him all pain and fear.

Say, "God wills that I be saved from this,"
and rest saved and safe forever in His Arms.

Sweet dreams of Awakening

235

Good Night, Will of God.

The power of decision is your own.
Choose to follow in Your Father's Footsteps,
and your life is filled with Love and Light,
Peace and Joy, Innocence and Freedom.

Offer your will to Him and discover
His Will is yours for the Kingdom of Heaven
is within you and you are within the Kingdom of Heaven.

Sweet dreams of Awakening

Good Night, God's Creation.

Tonight, accept the Truth about your Self.
Behold the world that Christ would have you see,
joyfully gleaming beyond the bitter dream of death.

Receive glad tidings of salvation as you sleep and
tomorrow rise in glory to shine your Light
upon the world and all your brothers
who are One with you.

Sweet dreams of Awakening

Good Night, Worthy Soul.

You are beloved of your Father indeed.
And He trusts you hold your brothers just as worthy.
As you drift to sleep, let your mind be saturated
with how much Your Father loves you
and how you are made complete in Him.

Sweet dreams of Awakening

Good Night, God's Glory.

Let us pray: "We thank you, Father,
for the Light that shines forever in us.
And we honor this Light, because You share It with us.
We are One, united in this Light and One with You,
at peace with all creation and our Self. Amen."

Sweet dreams of Awakening

239

Good Night, Fearless Freedom.

You are an extension of Fearlessness Itself!
God created you as Love, and Love is Fearless and Free.

Faith helps you see that God's Son is EveryOne.
Forgive your brothers in Your Father's Nameless Name,
that you may understand His Holiness, and Your Own.

Sweet dreams of Awakening

240

Good Night, Prodigal Child.

This holy instant choose to melt into the Heart of God.
Truly forgiving one brother releases all brothers,
and then you come to know yourself as forgiven.

Forgiveness is salvation, unconditional and unifying.
Trust it is safe to nestle in Your Father's Loving Arms,
and waken with the dawn to a world set free.

Sweet dreams of Awakening

Good Night, God's Gift.

What you give God, He gives you
a thousand times and more.

Come to Him tonight with a wholly open mind.
Let Him enfold you in His Sweet Embrace
and surrender your ideas to One Who
knows you better than you know yourself.

Humbly accept His Gift and be guided Home.

Sweet dreams of Awakening

242

Good Night, Holy Creation.

Tonight, drop all judgments and be honest with yourself.
You cannot understand what is beyond your present grasp.
In this humility shines resplendent freedom.

Honor every part of creation,
in which you are included, whole and holy,
and receive the Shining Truth of your Self as you sleep.

Sweet dreams of Awakening

243

Good Night, Same Name.

There can be no danger when
you tuck yourself under Your Father's Wing.

You have inherited His Name,
and with that comes the invulnerability of Oneness.

Storms cannot enter the mind which receives His Grace.
Rest you safely within His Embrace.

Sweet dreams of Awakening

Good Night, Peacekeeper.

*Your Father's Peace surrounds you and
keeps you safe from imaginary nightmares
in which you no longer need believe.*

*Accept His Wordless Word and confirm this for yourself
by requesting He send you the hopeless and unhappy.
As you quietly shine His Light on everyone you meet
you strengthen your conviction in Truth and Peace,
while humbly keeping your head at His Lotus Feet.*

Sweet dreams of Awakening

245

Good Night, Pure Love.

Know that your Father loves you,
and if you are loved then you are Love Itself.
Rest your head on your Father's Shoulder
as He hums a holy lullaby in your ear.
Drift to sleep as He calmly restores your Love.

Sweet dreams of Awakening

246

Good Night, Forgiven One.

Gaze into Your Father's Face
and feel the Love He has for you.
You were blind, but now you see that
You are Innocent, Formless, Unified Oneness.

God's Loveliness but reflects your own.
Let the body's eyes grow heavy
as Your Spiritual Eye opens wide.

Sweet dreams of Awakening

Good Night, Ancient Love.

Your Father's ancient love for you
lives outside of time and space in Holy Beingness.
You are as He created you! Timeless, Infinite, and Free.

Feel Him clasp you to His Heart.
Now, sleep this night Pure and Holy.

Sweet dreams of Awakening

Good Night, Child of God.

*The time has come to return your mind
to Your Father, and, in so doing, encounter the real world
where Life is joy, abundance, and endless giving.*

*The journey undertaken by you, Child of God,
ends in the Light from which it came.
Rest you again in Him, as He created You.*

Sweet dreams of Awakening

249

Good Night, Limitless Light.

Lay yourself down in the cradle of Your Father's Arms and feel His Unlimited Strength and Gentleness.

Release every fear and all tension into His care and be comforted by the remembrance of the Light You Are.

Sweet dreams of Awakening

Good Night, One Truth.

You sought for many things and found despair.
Now the truth dawns: you did not need anything but Love.

Close your eyes and open your mind
to Your Father's Nurturing Embrace.
From here, your Spiritual Eye reveals
that Truth and Love are the Same.
In this awareness are **all** needs satisfied.

Sweet dreams of Awakening

Good Night, Boundless Love.

You and Your Father are very close.
Snuggle up with Him tonight and
feel the calm intensity which is your true Self.

You shimmer with a perfect purity far more
brilliant than any light you have ever looked upon.
His Quiet Certainty and Boundless Love is your Identity.

Sweet dreams of Awakening

Good Night, Holy Self.

You are the master of your destiny:
You get to choose the separate self or the Holy Self.
As a separate self you are merely
a person packaged in a body.
As the Holy Self you are ruler of the universe.

Acknowledge You are joined in perfect union
with your Creator and every single brother and
your Limitless Nature and Universal Love prevail.

Sweet dreams of Awakening

Good Night, True Stillness.

*Tonight, come in deepest silence to hear God's Voice
and to receive His Word. Release all ego thoughts
and choose only God's Direct Truth.*

*Let every voice but God's be still in you.
And in this stillness, hallowed by His Love,
God sweeps you up and shines His Will through You.*

Sweet dreams of Awakening

254

Good Night, Perfect Peace.

It does not seem to you that you are Perfect Peace.
Yet Your Father wills that it is so.
Therefore, do not argue or protest.
Instead, choose to pass this night with Your Father
basking in your birthright and your legacy.

Sweet dreams of Awakening

255

Good Night, Sacred Word.

Tonight, choose to see your brothers
and yourself as Innocent. This Innocence has nothing to do
with actions; it is the Innocence of One-Minded Wholeness.

God is your only goal and forgiveness is the means
by which your mind returns to Him, as you listen
to the Inner Voice which speaks His Sacred Word.

Sweet dreams of Awakening

Good Night, Unified Purpose.

*Let us pray: "Father, forgiveness is Your chosen means
for my salvation. I am saved from fear and loneliness
when I remember there is no will but Yours.
Thus my purpose must be Yours as well,
to reach the peace You Will for me.*

*Thank you for using my sleep to unify
my thoughts with Yours. Namaste."*

Sweet dreams of Awakening

257

Good Night, God's Grace.

Stop pining for the toys and trinkets of this world.
The happiness they bring is temporary at best.
Instead, allow God's Grace to shine in your awareness,
for in this Light all your needs are Answered.

Tonight, let God be your only goal, your only Love.
Your heart will overflow with peace and certainty
as you allow grace to show you that you are Love.

Sweet dreams of Awakening

Good Night, Sweet Innocence.

You have not sinned and have no need for guilt.
Let your conscience be clear as you give every hurt
and each regret to the Holy Spirit to purify for you.

Love can have no opposite and You are Love Itself.
Now snuggle up to Your Father, certain all is well.

Sweet dreams of Awakening

259

Good Night, Dear Self.

Now is your Source remembered,
and Therein your true Identity found at last.
Truth dawns that you are as God created you!
Tonight sleep tight, safe and sound, as One Self
in One Heart where the Father and Son are joined forever.

Sweet dreams of Awakening

Good Night, Invulnerable One.

God's Embrace is your refuge and security.
You live in Him. Lay your head on His Shoulder
and rest in His everlasting peace as you sleep,
recognizing, indisputably, What you really are.

Sweet dreams of Awakening

Good Night, Same Name.

Your Father is part of you, and you of Him.
All God's Children share the Same Name
and are eternally united in Fatherly Love.

Let's all snuggle up to Our Shared Source
and gladly accept that we are One.
Relax into the safe coziness and warm security
of your Holy Family.

Sweet dreams of Awakening

Good Night, Holy Purity.

Your Father created all that is, and His Spirit is your Spirit.
His Love gave Life to you, and you are blessed
with His Purity, Innocence and Joy.

Tonight, He Quietly walks you Home;
do not drop His Hand at Heaven's Gate.

Sweet dreams of Awakening

Good Night, Love of God.

Your Father stands before you and behind you,
beside you, and between you and your brother.

He is everywhere you go for He is in you.
In Him time disappears and place becomes
a meaningless belief. You are surrounded
by the Love of God. Exalt in this Truth tonight!

Sweet dreams of Awakening

Good Night, Gentle One.

Tonight, rest in a world of gentle Stillness where celestial Innocence and Sanity shine eternally.

The ferocity of ego madness cannot withstand the Love of God. Sleep tranquilly in His Heavenly Light.

Sweet dreams of Awakening

Good Night, Paradise Found.

Every person who crosses your path
has the spark of God's Light within them, as do you.

Choose to see the Holy Self we all share,
and recognize there are no others, only brothers.

This night enter into Paradise, hearing God call your Name
and realizing it is the Same Name for everyone.

Sweet dreams of Awakening

Good Night, One Heart.

You are a messenger of God, directed by His Voice,
sustained by Him in love, and held forever quiet
and at peace within His loving Spirit.

Each of your heartbeats calls His Name,
and every one is answered by His Voice.
Accept His assurance that you are Home
within the Peaceful Heart of His Fatherly Love.

Sweet dreams of Awakening

267

Good Night, True Unity.

In Love you were created, and in Love you remain forever.
It is all right to let all things be exactly as they are.
There is a higher understanding you do not grasp right now.

Just know that you need do nothing but leave Unity
undisturbed. Heal in the holy truth of Love and
you need never be afraid or hurt again.

Sweet dreams of Awakening

Good Night, Blessed Self.

Tonight, choose to see a world forgiven,
in which every face shows you the face of Christ.

Release your thoughts so perception is replaced with Truth,
fear with Love, and conflict with Inner Peace.

See for yourself we share One Vision, One Name
and a blessed Face which is the Same.

Sweet dreams of Awakening

Good Night, God's Child.

Christ's Vision translates all that the body's eyes behold
into a gracious and glorious forgiven world!

Your willingness to forgive and be forgiven allows
bad dreams to be washed away in the Light of Truth.
Tonight, join your will with His and see through His Vision.

Sweet dreams of Awakening

Good Night, One Self.

*In Christ's Vision, the world and God's Creation meet,
and as they come together all perception disappears.
This eve, choose to look upon what Christ
would have you see; listen to God's Voice, and
let His kindly Vision remove the idea of death.*

*When you behold the truth with Your Self,
the memory of unending Life is restored to you.
Choose to look upon only this tonight.*

Sweet dreams of Awakening

271

Good Night, Heavenly One.

It is time to choose to live happily ever after.
Accept no less than what Your Father has given you,
and you will know you are surrounded by His Love,
forever still, forever gentle and forever safe.

Your Father tucks the covers around you
and whispers into your ear, "You are as I created you,
Formless, Free and forever Here with Me."

Sweet dreams of Awakening

Good Night, Tranquil One.

The stillness of the peace of God is yours.
You cannot lose Your Father's Gifts, though
you may have forgotten where they are.

Just repeat as you fall asleep tonight,
"The stillness of the peace of God is mine."
Now feel His Tranquility expand within you.

Sweet dreams of Awakening

Good Night, Fearless One.

Tonight, Your Father replaces darkness with Light,
illusions with Truth. Open to His Love and
accept the special blessings He showers upon You.

Give this night to Him and
your sleep is given unto Love.

Sweet dreams of Awakening

Good Night, Holy One.

Your Father's healing Voice protects you day and night.
You need be anxious over nothing because
He tells you what to do and where to go;
to whom to speak and what to say;
what thoughts to think, which words to give the world.
The safety that you need is given you to give away
that all brothers live unified in peace and harmony.

Sweet dreams of Awakening

Good Night, God's Word.

What is God's Word?
"My Child is pure and holy as Myself."

Accept His Word by saying, "Father, Your Word is mine.
And it is this that I would speak to all my brothers,
who are given me to cherish as my own,
as I am loved and blessed and saved by You."

Sweet dreams of Awakening

Good Night, Timeless Love.

You are not slave to any laws of time.
You are as Your Father created you, Timeless and Free,
because He knows no law except His Law of Love.

You are your Father's Child, so sleep carefree this night,
unbound from lying ego laws; liberated by Honest Truth.

Sweet dreams of Awakening

277

Good Night, Boundless One.

Ask your Father for nothing but the truth
and infinite joy ripples through your heart and mind.

You have had many foolish thoughts
about yourself, and have slept eons of troubled sleep.

Tonight, save yourself by choosing Him Who
liberates you from the prison of false ego ideas.
Truth is safe, and delivers only Eternal, Boundless Love.

Sweet dreams of Awakening

Good Night, God's Creation.

It's bedtime. Let your Father rock you gently in His Arms.
His Presence shines the Truth through your mind, and bad
dreams disappear as Heaven's Beauty appears in their place.

Now you realize Freedom has been yours all along.
Your heart sings a song of pure gratitude as you
lay down your chains and clasp What You really are.

Sweet dreams of Awakening

Good Night, Limitless One.

No Thought of God has left its Father's Mind,
and, as His Child, you are a Thought of God.

Your Father's Will is that you are limitless, pure and free.
In that freedom is your peace, love and joy.
Lay down **all** thoughts of limitation right now.

Sweet dreams of Awakening

Good Night, Perfection Itself.

You can only hurt when you think your own thoughts.
Join your mind with Your Father,
Who watches over you always.

Let Him think for you as you sleep tonight,
and be healed and blessed by His Perfect Love.

Sweet dreams of Awakening

281

Good Night, Loved One.

Let us pray: "Father, Your Name is Love
and, therefore, so is mine. Such is the truth.
Can the truth be changed by merely giving it another name?
The name of fear is simply a mistake.
Let me not be afraid of Love tonight.
Let me accept forever living in the Joy of Love.
Let me accept our One Identity. And so it is."

Sweet dreams of Awakening

Good Night, Light of Heaven.

Tonight, slumber in unity with your brothers,
filled with God's blessings and overflowing with His Love.

Heaven is bright with your Light,
and sleep is peaceful when your Mind is illuminated,
shining holiness endlessly, certain of your Infinite Identity.

Sweet dreams of Awakening

283

Good Night, Painless Truth.

Suffering of any kind is nothing but a dream.
This is the Truth, at first to be but said;
next, to be accepted as but partly true,
then to be considered seriously more and more,
and finally, accepted as the Truth.

*Release your belief in pain that **seems** obvious and real.*
Right now, give all hurt and suffering to the Holy Spirit,
and accept only His joyous gifts as the Truth.

Sweet dreams of Awakening

Good Night, Holy Vision.

Your Father kisses your eyelids
and Vision blazes through your mind.

Tonight, sleep with joy, expecting only
the happy Ideas of God to come to you.
For you are still as God created you.

Merely ask and be Answered with One brightly shining
Joyous Thought the instant you accept your holiness.

Sweet dreams of Awakening

Good Night, Heaven's Heart.

There is no need for you to do anything.
When you accept this, how quietly
do things fall into place.

In Your Father is everything you
hope to find already given you.
Merely step back and follow His Direction
and how quickly you encounter the hush of Heaven.

Sweet dreams of Awakening

286

Good Night, God's Child.

What gift could you prefer to the Peace of God?
What treasure could compare with your True Identity?
Would you deliberately choose fear over Love?

Place your cheek upon your Father's Chest
and surrender your heart to His.

Sweet dreams of Awakening

287

Good Night, Eternal Present.

Drop the past and take your brother's hand.
For as you do, you enter the ever-present Truth
that we all have One Holy Name.

Behind your sleeping eyes,
your brothers glow softly with the Unified
radiance shared by all who dare to truly see.

Sweet dreams of Awakening

Good Night, Sweet Forgiveness.

*Your Father strokes your brow, and
wipes away the past where you have been hiding.
Guilt is the glue that holds the ego together.
Look not upon people and personalities.*

*See through this illusion into the ineffable light
which is your true Self. Soften your heart
with sweet forgiveness for the whole world,
and soften your eyes to sleep with true Vision.*

Sweet dreams of Awakening

Good Night, Happy Dreamer.

No longer do you choose to be deceived
by ego dreams of suffering and separation.
Your Father wills that you be happy, joyful and free!

The dream you made has never been real,
but the Holy Spirit can use it to open your mind
if you invite Him to guide you.

Sweet dreams of Awakening

Good Night, Quiet Mind.

This eve your mind is quietly receiving God's Thoughts.
Accept what comes from Him, and moves through you,
as He Guides you along the quiet path that leads Home.

All is forgiven and lit with loveliness.
All is forgiven and pure with holiness.
All is awaiting your decision to enter this Stillness now.

Sweet dreams of Awakening

291

Good Night, Happy Outcome.

*Your Father promises you a happy outcome
for His Will is done in earth and Heaven
so long as you do not interfere.*

*Sink deeply under your covers
and have faith in His guarantee
of your Infinite Joy tonight.*

Sweet dreams of Awakening

Good Night, Present Love.

When you connect with your Father,
the world is bright and clear, welcoming and safe.

Let the soft starlight glow of evening
remind you that all the world shines
in the reflection of Love's Light.

Snuggle into your pillow and listen to
the holy hymns of gratitude that transcend
worldly sounds and lift you into God's Presence.

Sweet dreams of Awakening

293

Good Night, God's Child.

You are a Child of God. Therefore,
you cannot be a person in a body.

The body is not your true Self,
but while you think you are in the world,
it can be of service for a while.

Rest in your Father's Loving Arms this night,
and trust in His plan for your salvation.

Sweet dreams of Awakening

Good Night, Eyes of Christ.

Your Father asks you to allow the Holy Spirit's Love to bless all things you look upon, so that His forgiving Love is reflected back to you.

Let your eyes and ears and hands and feet offer peace to all you meet in your dreams tonight. Unwind, and see them through the Eyes of Christ.

Sweet dreams of Awakening

Good Night, God's Messenger.

God's Word flows through you night and day,
but it goes unheard unless you ask to hear It.

When you ask, and listen to His Voice within,
there are no words but His, and they emerge
from you effortlessly when you choose
to follow the Holy Spirit's Easy Path to God.

Sweet dreams of Awakening

Good Night, God's Grace.

It is time for bed and time for prayer:
"Father, how certain are Your ways,
how sure their final outcome, and
how faithfully is every step
in my salvation set already,
and accomplished by Your Grace.

Thanks be to You for Your eternal gifts,
and thanks to You for my Identity. Shalom."

Sweet dreams of Awakening

Good Night, Fearless Love.

Tonight, thank your Father for His certain sanctuary,
because He is always beside you and you are never alone.

Your gratitude releases you from fear.
As you accept His Love, boundaries dissolve,
and you are restored at last to unobscured Reality.
Free of fear, bask in His Light as the Love you are.

Sweet dreams of Awakening

Good Night, Holy Abidance.

Holiness created You and holiness You Are.
Nothing can change This.

Divinity is beyond human understanding,
which only proves Its Truth.

You remain forever Perfect and Untouched,
not as a person, but as Presence.

Open to your Divine Source tonight.

Sweet dreams of Awakening

Good Night, Cloudless Mind.

Spirit whispers a bedtime story in your heart:
a tale of how to go beyond the ego's tiny, mad idea
of time and space, and return to the serenity of Infinity.
God's Mind is your True Home, Cloudless and Serene.

Tonight, surrender and be swept above
the star-lit night into Exquisite Eternity.

Sweet dreams of Awakening

Good Night, Tears of Joy.

You wept because you did not
understand the truth about your Self.
Your Father would not have you suffer,
so He shows you how to see Life through His Eyes.

Drop all judgment and forgiveness reveals Love-Light in
everyone and everything, everywhere.
Drop the person completely and you are absorbed in
No-Body, No-Thing and No-Where.
Now, you can happily weep sparkling tears of Joy!

Sweet dreams of Awakening

Good Night, Holy Light.

Christ's vision changes darkness into Light,
for fear must disappear when Love has come.

Even in sleep, darkness is your own imagining,
and Light is here for you to look upon.

Attune your mind to your One Self
and be shown the way.

Sweet dreams of Awakening

302

Good Night, Anointed One.

Snuggle into Your Father's Safe and Loving Arms.
In His Presence earthly sounds grow quiet and
angels surround you with Stillness and Heavenly Love.

You become aware that all God's holy Thoughts
envelop you in His Heart, and it is impossible
that you be a stranger anywhere,
for you are the Christ Child,
as is Jesus and all your brothers.

Sweet dreams of Awakening

Good Night, Blessed One.

Your Father's gift to you is His Loving God-Mind.
Close your eyes and open to what comes naturally:
perceive through His Vision; connect with His Will.

Then you will know yourself as Perfect Peace and Joy;
then you will know your brothers as your Self.

Sweet dreams of Awakening

Good Night, Healed Mind.

It is Your Father's Will that you be saved
from fearful thoughts and blinding ego sleep.

He Wills that you accept His Gift:
a peace so deep and quiet,
Undisturbable and wholly Changeless
that the world you perceive evaporates
in the Wisdom of the Infinite, for Love has come.

Sweet dreams of Awakening

305

Good Night, Gifted One.

Let us pray: "Our Father,
tonight we return to You,
remembering we never went away.
The ancient memory of Your holy gifts
of Love, Kindness, Peace and Joy is restored to us.

In gratitude and thankfulness we come,
with empty hands, and open hearts and minds,
asking only for what You give, and giving freely
what is Received. And so it is."

Sweet dreams of Awakening

Good Night, Willing One.

Lay your head on your pillow and open your mind to Truth.
This Truth is Silent Stillness, ever peaceful,
where conflict cannot come.

Here, you, your brothers and Your Father are One, in Being
and in Will, because you remain as God created you.
Tonight, join your holy will with God's,
in recognition that they are the Same.

Sweet dreams of Awakening

Good Night, Timeless One.

Are you willing to change your perception
of what time is for? Elect to reach past time to
Timelessness, and discover Who you really are.

Jesus comes without a past or future to give you
and the entire world His present blessing.
When you accept this blessing,
Timelessness and Love are restored to your awareness
and Love is ever-present, here and now.

Sweet dreams of Awakening

308

Good Night, Eternal Innocence.

Within you is the holiness of God.
Within you is the memory of Him.
Within you is the Self that God created,
the Fearless Guilt-free Self you are in Truth.

This eve, look within and find the Oneness in which
true Harmony and Innocence timelessly abides as You.

Sweet dreams of Awakening

309

Good Night, Fearless One.

Spend this night with Your Father,
accepting His Will as your own.
In this way are you restored to sweetness and serenity.
In this way, fear is replaced by Love.

Give thanks for the spark of grace
within us all which is your Christ Face.
In True Identity there is no room for fear
since you have welcomed Love into your heart.

Sweet dreams of Awakening

Good Night, Innocent Love.

Your Father wants to relieve you
of the agony of all the judgments
you have made against yourself and others.

This evening rest with an open mind,
absorbing God's Judgment which
is always Unconditional Love.

You are as God created you.
Receive His Gift and rest assured.

Sweet dreams of Awakening

311

Good Night, Holy Sight.

Take the Holy Spirit's purpose as your own
and see a liberated world, set free from judgment.

Simply elect all-encompassing Love to filter through
your sleeping mind, purifying and evaporating
every frightening or unloving thought you ever had.

Sweet dreams of Awakening

Good Night, Holy Light.

Tonight, see yourself as Your Father sees you.
How beautiful you are! How innocent and loving!
Holy Child, in God's Vision you are as pure and lovable
as the Holy Light which is the essence of everyone.

Open to true perception and recognize this truth,
this very eve, this very moment, now.

Sweet dreams of Awakening

313

Good Night, Beloved Seeker.

Place the future in your Father's Hands
and leave behind your past mistakes.

Now is the time for seeking to come to an end,
and you will find the present extends Bodiless Freedom,
Timeless Tranquility, Personless Love and Limitless Joy.

Live in the Light which casts no shadows!

Sweet dreams of Awakening

Good Night, Priceless Treasure.

This night a thousand treasures come to you,
Who is Treasure Itself. Smile upon your brother and
receive the gift of Eternal Radiance reflected back to you.

You are blessed with the priceless treasure of Being,
far beyond anything of which the ego can conceive.
Just say "Thank you," and graciously accept
the Limitless Gift which is your birthright.

Sweet dreams of Awakening

315

Good Night, Treasured Soul.

Your treasure house is full,
and yet angels continue to add more.

Each gift you give allows a past mistake to go,
and leaves no shadow on the Holy Mind God loves.

Enter in where you are truly welcome and at Home,
among the Formless Gifts that God has given you.

Sweet dreams of Awakening

316

Good Night, Appointed One.

Your Father's way is certain and the end secure.
The present memory of Him awaits you Here.

All your sorrows end in His Firm Embrace,
though you thought you had wandered away
from the sure protection of His Devoted Arms.

Willingly choose to accept His Plan
and salvation is yours tonight.

Sweet dreams of Awakening

317

Good Night, One Purpose.

Your Father's one request is that you
accept salvation and Atonement for yourself.

When you do so, your purpose is fulfilled.
You discover you are what you are seeking for:
One All-Inclusive Love, Endlessly Extending.

Go within and see you are salvation's means and end.
Elect, now, to uncover God's Creation which is Your Self.

Sweet dreams of Awakening

Good Night, Sweet Humility.

Your Father sees you as Whole and Perfect because His Vision created you Spacious, Formless and True.

It is ego arrogance to believe you are a person when you are truly an extension of His Great Rays.

Undo the limited self-concept that keeps you imprisoned by unconscious lies. Devote your sleeping hours tonight to humbly connecting your will with His.

Sweet dreams of Awakening

Good Night, One and Only.

God's Only Child is Limitless.
Your Creator and Redeemer places no limits
on your strength, your peace, your joy,
nor any attributes your Father gave in your Creation.

You are The One in whom the power
of your Father's Will abides.
And His Will can be used for Love and only Love.
Tonight, accept His Power as your own.

Sweet dreams of Awakening

Good Night, Freedom Rider.

Only when you let Your Father's Voice direct you,
do you find your way to Freedom.

The way to Him is opening and clear to you at last,
as you step back and let Him lead the way.
Liberation is here for you this very night.

Sweet dreams of Awakening

Good Night, Dream Weaver.

The ego dreams to conceal the Self
which is God's only Child. That One is you.

There is no loss except the loss of fear
when you accept God's ancient shining Message
of Love and Unity. You are still the Holy One,
Who abides in Him forever.

Give ego dreams to the Holy Spirit,
Who uses them to reveal the True You.

Sweet dreams of Awakening

Good Night, Beloved Child.

The only "sacrifice" God asks of you is that you give up all suffering, anxiety, doubt, shame and sadness.

In return, receive His Truth streaming into your awareness, restoring you to Immortal Sanity, and the Ceaseless Love and Joy that is God-Mind.

Freely allow Your Father's Love to flow full force into your heart and know what it is to be Beloved.

Sweet dreams of Awakening

323

Good Night, Fellow Follower.

Let us follow One Who knows the way.
Though you chose to wander off for a while,
you cannot stray but an instant from His Guiding Hand.

Lifetimes of dreams are undone as you follow Him
Who makes the ending sure, and guarantees
a safe and heavenly return Home.

Sweet dreams of Awakening

324

Good Night, Perfect Idea.

Let us pray: "Father, Your Ideas reflect Reality,
and ours apart from Yours but make up dreams.
Let us behold what only Your Ideas reflect,
for Yours and Yours alone establish Truth.
From forgiving thoughts comes forth a gentle world.
This very night would we walk Home
with our brothers to You. Ashay!"

Sweet dreams of Awakening

Good Night, Holy Thought.

You are forever God's Effect, for He is your Cause.
Tonight, follow Your Father's Plan,
using only His power to co-create.
As you recognize the Love you are,
behold the earth disappear, and watch
all separate thoughts unite in glory
as One Holy Thought of Sonship.

Sweet dreams of Awakening

326

Good Night, Faithful One.

If you but call His Name, He will come.

Your Father does not test you;
He but asks that you test Him.
For He has promised to Answer your call
and experience proves that He has not abandoned you.

Strengthen your faith by softening into His Abiding Love.
Conviction comes as you accept His Word.

Sweet dreams of Awakening

327

Good Night, Second One.

Jesus followed the Holy Spirit and
discovered there is no point at which
the Father ends and the Son begins.

The Creator and His Creation naturally merge
as Divine Abstraction and Sublime Formlessness.
Tonight, choose second place and gain God's Autonomy.

Sweet dreams of Awakening

328

Good Night, God's Will.

As Your Father is One, so are you One with Him.
Your Father's Will is yours, and what you are in truth
is but His Will, eternally extended and extending.

Tonight, willingly turn your face towards His
and joyously accept Union with your Source.

Sweet dreams of Awakening

Good Night, One Identity.

This night escape forever from all things
the ego dream of fear appears to offer you.

Be willing to be saved from the person
you think you are and allow your mind
to be restored to Spirit-Mind, your true Identity.

God holds out His Power and His Love
and bids you take what is already Yours.

Sweet dreams of Awakening

Good Night, Peaceful One.

How could you think that Love has left Itself?
God Wills only Harmony, and there is no will but His.

Bad dreams end forever as you realize the
decision to awaken delivers eternal peace of mind.

Forgiveness unveils the illusion that your will is separate
from God's. Surrender "your will" to His and find
One Peace is yours, tonight.

Sweet dreams of Awakening

331

Good Night, Liberated One.

Truth undoes loveless dreams by shining them away.
And by Truth's Presence is the ego mind
recalled from fantasies, awaking to the Real.

Without forgiveness is the mind in chains,
trapped in a self-made dream of darkness.
Tonight, accept the Light Your Father offers
and set yourself and the whole world free.

Sweet dreams of Awakening

332

Good Night, Shining Truth.

If it would be resolved,
conflict must be seen for what it is.
Be steadfastly honest and look openly
with the Holy Spirit at what the ego made.

Your self-concept is deceitful by nature,
so let forgiveness remove all lies and then the
Shining Truth within you vividly illuminates the path Home.

Sweet dreams of Awakening

333

Good Night, Treasured One.

Ego dreams rely on false perception
and have no foundation whatsoever.
Give them meaning by giving them to the Holy Spirit
and He will use them for His transcendent purpose.

This is your choice tonight. Ego or Eternal.
Wait no more. Seek only the Eternal and
find the Timeless Treasure God gives you forevermore.

Sweet dreams of Awakening

334

Good Night, Pure Innocence.

*Your yearning to be cradled in Your Father's Arms
can be fulfilled simply by recognizing your Sinless Purity.*

*No matter what you think of yourself, or another,
be willing to see the Innocence
that is the essence of every person.*

*In this way, discover the holiness
that created you One with All.*

Sweet dreams of Awakening

335

Good Night, Abiding Love.

Snuggle up to Your Father
and let your mind grow quiet.
May His lilies of forgiveness shine away
all dreams of separation and sin.

Look within with Him, and find His Word
remains unchanged within your mind, for
His Love always abides inside your Heart.

Sweet dreams of Awakening

Good Night, Perfect Peace.

As you lay down to sleep, remember
you need do nothing except
not to interfere with God's Love for you.

As you accept His Love, you notice
*you **are** happy, safe, peaceful and free*
no matter what your circumstances.

Your Father kisses your eyelids to
free you forever from old nightmares.

Sweet dreams of Awakening

337

Good Night, One Thought.

*You have the power to change your thoughts and
release yourself from the belief in the external world.*

*Give Your Father every thought you think
as you fall asleep tonight. He will gladly smooth your brow
and exchange each fear for His Happy Thought of Love.*

Sweet dreams of Awakening

338

Good Night, Receptive One.

*Let us pray: "Father, we give this night
to You to listen to Your Voice.
Help us request only
what You would offer us.*

*We have been confused and mistook pain for joy and
fear for love. Father, as we sleep tonight we choose
to tune in to Your Voice and see with Your Vision.
Thank you and Aloha."*

Sweet dreams of Awakening

Good Night, Heart of Love.

Be glad this evening and give thanks!
Your Father gathers you in His Arms
so you can fall asleep with your cheek
against His Chest. Feel all your fears melt
away as you securely rest in His Heart of Love.

Sweet dreams of Awakening

Good Night, Holy One.

Gaze into Your Father's Face and
see how tenderly He Smiles at you!

Give in to His Love and feel how pure,
how innocent, how holy you truly are.
Your Sinlessness ensures your safety;
your Innocence ensures His Grace.

Abide in this Holiness and the
entire universe smiles on you.

Sweet dreams of Awakening

Good Night, Blazing Light.

The key to Heaven is in your hand,
and you have reached the gate beyond which
lies the end of all dreams. Wait no longer.

Unlock the memory of your true Identity
by opening the door at last, and watch illusions
be consumed in the blazing Light of Truth.

Sweet dreams of Awakening

342

Good Night, Overflowing Abundance.

*Your Father's Nature is overflowing abundance,
unconditionally and completely given to you, His Child.*

*His Law is that giving is receiving.
His legacy is that you receive and extend
what He has given you forever and forever.
Tonight, claim your Inheritance:
Receive His Boundless Treasure tonight.*

Sweet dreams of Awakening

343

Good Night, Treasured One.

The Law of Love is fulfilled when you forgive.
Then your heart overflows with Heaven's Treasures
which hold gifts far beyond the ego's meager imaginings.

God is nearer than your very breath.
Admit this and He welcomes you to the
Treasured Land which is your rightful Home.

Sweet dreams of Awakening

344

Good Night, Universal Love.

The Law of Love is universal:
what you give you must receive.

Each miracle you give returns to you
a thousandfold and more
if you accept them!

Receive the Unifying Love
God offers you to give your brothers
and rest unceasingly in His Grace.

Sweet dreams of Awakening

345

Good Night, Miracle Worker.

Tonight, forget all things but Your Father's Love.
Allow the Peace of God to envelop you completely.

This holy instant step beyond time and abide in Him,
Whose miracles heal all misperceptions as you sleep.
In the morning, the world shall be transformed.

Sweet dreams of Awakening

Good Night, Pure Innocence.

Listen tonight. Be very still, and hear
the gentle Voice for God assuring you that
He has judged you Innocent
for you are His Beloved Child.

Bad dreams hid miracles from your awareness,
but this eve, let Your Father straighten your mind and
reveal Purity to you as you surrender your will to His.

Sweet dreams of Awakening

347

Good Night, Perfect Holiness.

God's Grace is yours. You discover this is true
when you place your fear and anger at His Feet.

Unburdened of guilt and judgment, discover that
He created you in holiness as perfect as His Own.

Accept His eternal promise that you are surrounded
by Perfect Peace, Love and Joy, and feel His Arms
tenderly encircle you in Everlasting Safety.

Sweet dreams of Awakening

348

Good Night, Miraculous One.

Your Father knows you better
than you know yourself.

Help Him heal you by praying:
"Father, your gifts are mine.
Each one that I accept
gives me a miracle to give.
And giving as I would receive,
I learn Your miracles of love belong to me."

Trust in Him to bless you and the whole world,
tonight and every night.

Sweet dreams of Awakening

349

Good Night, Eternal Love.

Turn to Your Father tonight and
choose to remember what you deliberately forgot.

Remain unconscious no longer.
The memory of God returns to your mind
as you forgive, and sets you free!

Miracles mirror Your Father's Eternal Love.
To offer miracles is to remember God and
that you and all your brothers are One.

Sweet dreams of Awakening

Good Night, Holy Child.

All relationships can be used for healing.
The essence of all humanity is the Light of God.

Choose to see beyond personalities
and find Your Whole and Holy Self.

Accept the guidance of the Holy Spirit,
your Comforter and Friend, Who will
gladly show you how, now.

Sweet dreams of Awakening

351

Good Night, Peaceful Identity.

You have within you both the memory of God
and the One Who leads you to this memory.

Hear Your Father's Voice
and find Your peace tonight.

Love, reflected in forgiveness here,
would never leave you comfortless
and always gives you a way to find
God's peace, if only you ask.

Sweet dreams of Awakening

Good Night, Blessed One.

Tonight, your eyes, your tongue, your hands, your feet
have but one purpose: to be used by the Holy Spirit
to bless the world with miracles.

Now your heart gentles, your eyes soften,
your tongue rests from words.

Now your feet float across the starlit sky
until you meet your Self right here.

Sweet dreams of Awakening

353

Good Night, One Self.

You, your brothers and sisters,
and the Holy Spirit are all the Same One.

What seemed to be many is simply an illusion.
We are all beyond the reach of time and form,
and free of every law but God's.

God's Law remains Timelessly Loving
in Unified Harmony, always.
Be soothed by this Truth tonight.

Sweet dreams of Awakening

354

Good Night, God's Word.

Wait not an instant longer
for the Joy Your Father promised you.

Accept God's Word and discover your native tongue,
the Language of Love, Harmony and Beauty.

His Word is written on your heart;
look within and choose to be your Self.

Sweet dreams of Awakening

355

Good Night, God's Name.

Tonight, be cured of your case
of mistaken identity.
Gaze into the reflection
of Love and see your Self.

No matter what seems to be the problem,
all that matters is that you accept
God's Name as Your Own
and claim the miracles of Love
that every mind that has wandered
from Its Source.

Sweet dreams of Awakening

356

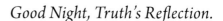

Good Night, Truth's Reflection.

*When you choose to behold another's Innocence,
you perceive yourself as Innocent and Whole.*

*Tonight, forgive your brothers, forgive yourself, and
forgive God by accepting His reflection in your mind.*

*Give in to His Voice which instructs you to:
"Behold Innocence in all and be you healed."*

Sweet dreams of Awakening

Good Night, Unforgettable One.

Let us pray: "Father, help me remember
all I do not know, and let my voice be still, remembering.
And let me not forget Your Love,
keeping Your promise to me in my awareness, always.

Most important, let me not forget myself is nothing,
but my Self is all. And so it is."

Sweet dreams of Awakening

358

Good Night, Inner Light.

What God created sinless so abides
forever and forever. Such are you.

God's Answer heals all pain and
replaces misery with Joy.
Prison doors are opened.
And all sin is understood as
merely a mistake in your mind.

Tonight, invite forgiveness to undo the shadow world
you convinced yourself is real and bask in your Inner Light.

Sweet dreams of Awakening

359

Good Night, Great Rays.

God's Great Rays remain forever still and
undisturbed within you. Your Inner Light is
created in holiness; and remains Infinite and Timeless.

Reach to these Great Rays of Light in certainty,
for they live inside you always.
Know this as true and gladly say, "Aho!"

Sweet dreams of Awakening

360

Good Night, God's Creation.

If you need a word to help you,
God will give It to you.

Simply choose to give this holy instant
to Him to be in charge. Follow Him,
certain that His Direction gives you peace.

For you are His Creation, and have inherited
His Qualities, if you but claim them.

Sweet dreams of Awakening

361

Good Night, Constant Peace.

As you lay your cheek on your pillow, remember:
If you need a tranquil Thought,
this Your Father gladly gives.

Offer Him your willing, open mind
and His Gifts you surely receive.

Sweet dreams of Awakening

Good Night, Immortal Mind.

*Your Father wills you live forever
and helps you understand this very night
that you and all your brothers are Immortality Itself.*

*Accept your Innocence and accept God's blessing
which changes the very purpose of your sleep.*

Sweet dreams of Awakening

363

Good Night, Divine Legacy.

God is in charge by your request.
Be not falsely humble, but instead
dare to accept your Divine Legacy.

This holy instant, use your power of decision
and choose to follow Your Source!
He gives you Everything if you but ask for No Thing.

Sweet dreams of Awakening

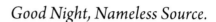

Good Night, Nameless Source.

This holy instant do you give to God.
Put Him in charge. For you would follow Him,
certain that His Direction gives you Peace.

Tonight, let it be known inside you
that the Nameless is Your Name
and that Your Source is You.

Come with empty hands and
open heart to meet your Self.

Sweet dreams of Awakening

365

"For we go homeward to an open door
which God has held unclosed to welcome us."

~A Course in Miracles

CPSIA information can be obtained
at www.ICGtesting.com
Printed in the USA
LVOW11s2124210817
545810LV00003B/700/P